Guide to Precious Metals and their Markets

Price analysis based on $100 investment between 1972-1977 in the following: Gold share price index, Gold, Silver, Platinum, Deutsche Mark, Japanese Yen, Pound Sterling, Dow Jones Industrial Average and Financial Times Share Index

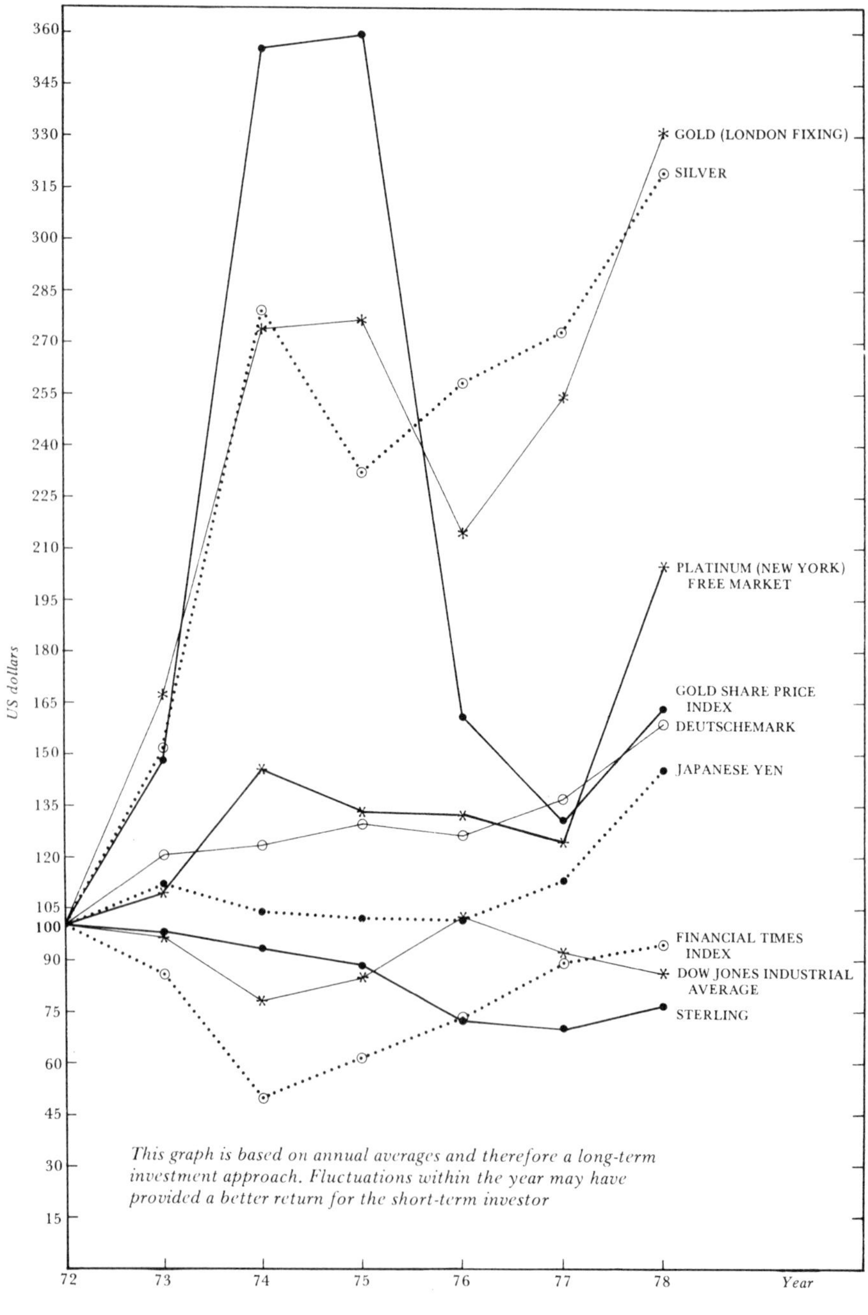

Contents

Part 5: Platinum group metals 75-107

Part 6: Metallurgy 109-113

Recent developments 115-117

Appendices 119-191

Tables, Graphs and Bar charts

**table **graph †bar chart*

**table* ***graph* *†bar chart*

**table* ***graph* †*bar chart*

Acknowledgements

The Authors would like to record their thanks for the help provided in preparing this book to Ethel de Keyser and David Young of Kogan Page, and to Tom Butler, Steve White and Brian Tweedie for providing useful information.

Part 1: Introduction

Introduction

Background to the markets

Precious metals are considered beautiful. They are also scarce and unique among commodities in that they are judged as a measure of wealth.

The important precious metals markets are exceedingly complex. Simple laws of supply and demand govern the markets of most commodities but precious metal markets are distorted by a number of inter-related factors. The more obvious of these are as follows:

- ☐ Gold has the most direct link with the monetary system but precious metal dealers have been inclined to believe in a close connection between the gold price and the prices of other precious metals. This view is justified to a certain extent because gold and other precious metals have many characteristics in common, including historical association, scarcity, uses (jewellery, electronics, etc), easy storage and in most cases similar origin.
- ☐ Most precious metals are produced as by-products or co-products of the manufacture of other, less rare, metals. In the event of a metal such as platinum being in great demand, when there is a low demand for nickel, a platinum producer may not be in a position to increase production if platinum is produced as a by-product of nickel at that particular mine.
- ☐ Industrial uses for precious metals are mostly as components in highly sophisticated areas of technology, where the value of the metal in the equipment or system may be insignificant. This means that, in many cases, a manufacturer is forced to buy the metal at almost any price because of its unique and unsubstitutable properties.
- ☐ The fact that the Soviet Union and South Africa account for the production of more than half the world's precious metals – the exception is silver – means that politics play a much greater role in the precious metals markets than in other commodity markets. In Britain, the Labour government, for instance curtailed the importation of gold coins from South Africa (this restraint was relaxed in the June 1979 budget under the new Conservative Government) and there is much debate in world centres on the

question of including gold in the monetary system since it benefits these two countries.

- All the precious metals are used in the manufacture of jewellery, demand for which is very much dependent upon the vagaries of fashion and taste. In Japan, for instance, platinum is considered more beautiful than gold because of its contrast in colour with oriental skin tones.
- Precious metals, historically, have demonstrated an ability to retain their value even in periods of extreme economic dislocation. In the present climate of economic uncertainty investors, both small and large, are worried about protecting their wealth, although much of this anxiety may be unjustified and ill-informed. Precious metals have become an important feature of investment portfolios. Governments are not enthusiastic about this type of investment as it tends to reduce the pool of money available for investment in industry. If investment in precious metals were to grow substantially, steps may be taken to discourage it, especially if this results in industry having to pay a much higher price for precious metal supplies.

Precious metals have important physical characteristics which make them indispensable to modern industry. This is illustrated by the following examples: one cubic centimetre of palladium is capable of absorbing 900cc of hydrogen; silver has the highest electrical conductivity of any metal; gold is the most ductile metal and one gram of it can be drawn into a wire 2,300 metres long; iridium is the most corrosion-resistant of all elements; osmium is the heaviest metal; and the platinum group contains the hardest metals.

This book attempts to notate and explain the major influences on these unique markets and to point out their common features. This last exercise is necessary, not only because of the influence one precious metal market has on the others, but also because these metals have certain physical properties in common which often means that one can be substituted for, or alloyed with, another, if price differentials so dictate.

Investors should not be tempted to enter these markets without making a serious commitment to study the day-to-day factors which influence prices. Advice needs to be sought from experts in the field and links made with dealing companies since, in volatile conditions, speedy decisions are necessary.

Industrial consumers of precious metals have unusually difficult problems in assessing market trends because of the complexity of these markets. However, they have a number of different ways of obtaining supplies, though the major choice is between the free market and the producers. For many of these metals the producers use a producer price system and at times this price may be much higher than that on the free market. Despite this factor, when continuity of supply and quality is of supreme importance, a consumer is more likely to obtain supplies from one or more producers.

The free market, as expressed through the prices arrived at by one or other of the formal precious metal markets or by informal dealings and fixings between precious metal merchants, moves more erratically than the producer price but represents a more accurate reflection of all the market forces. These markets also provide a hedging medium for both consumers and producers.

The future

The dramatic rise in price for all the major precious metals in 1978-79 is attributable to the growth in industrial demand; increased production costs; low production in previous years; rising inflation and, in the case of the platinum group metals, to reduced Russian exports.

It appears that, in spite of the official demonetization of gold, the habits of 6000 years die hard. Private individuals, banks, financial institutions and even governments retain sufficient faith in the intrinsic value of gold, and in its ability to compete with other forms of investment. Thus gold is still unofficially monetized, and is likely to remain a strong and active market for the forseeable future.

However, in spite of its great popularity in jewellery, gold consumption is not sufficiently industrially based to justify higher prices should the world's economy improve.

The future of gold is integrally bound up with the political prospects in Southern Africa and vice-versa. Any major dislocation of gold production in South Africa would not now undermine the world's monetary system but it would dramatically increase gold prices.

The IMF and the US Treasury have both reduced the rate of gold sales to the world market to a point where future decreases are unlikely to affect the market. In the present industrial and economic conditions producers are confident of further price rises but not perhaps at the rate current in 1978-79.

Some experts also feel that the high gold price might encourage exports from the USSR to be resumed, which would have the effect of reducing prices.

Industrial demand for silver is firmly based at present price levels but any price prediction exceeding the rate of world inflation is questionable. Substitution for silver, especially in photography, would become more viable at high price levels. Higher prices for the metals in which silver is found as a by-product will stimulate increased mine production and, since silver production is so widely based, supply disruption in any isolated area should not make any great impact on the market.

The Indian Government's policy on silver exports is likely to remain rigid while their economy continues to improve. However, the threat remains, that vast quantities of 'above ground' silver stocks in India may be released slowly onto the market if foreign currency is needed or if the country is economically strong and it is decided to relax export restrictions. This possibility casts doubt on the ability of silver to provide a good hedge against inflation, particularly since it is more dependent on industrial demand than either gold or platinum.

Pollution control is not as high a priority today as it was in the early 70's and the use of platinum for this purpose may not rise in future at the same rate. The powerful 'pollution lobby' in the United States has two major arguments to confront. First, can the rising platinum import bill be justified when balance of payments deficits need to be reduced, and second, how dependent does the United States wish to be on supplies from the Soviet Union and South Africa.

No clear reason has yet emerged for the sudden and dramatic reduction of platinum group metal exports from the USSR. Suggestions of mining problems or mines running out have been dismissed by the USSR, but these are still considered to be the most likely explanations by some experts. Others suggest that, since the Russian harvests have been improving, the need for foreign exchange is less acute. It is also worth mentioning that the USSR has imported vast quantities of tungsten in the last two years (despite the fact that it is one of the world's largest producers of that metal); that it has bought particularly large quantities of lead, alumina and cobalt; and that chrome exports have been virtually suspended. The explanation may be either that the USSR is building a strategic stockpile of these metals or that domestic consumption has risen sufficiently to absorb such quantities.

In any event, if this situation proves to be a continuing feature of the platinum group metal markets, prices must continue to rise substantially as South Africa alone may have neither the will nor the capacity to supply the entire world's requirements, and would prefer to let rising prices limit consumption.

No country, not even South Africa can replace the Soviet Union as a supplier of palladium. And since the Russians produce twice as much palladium as they do platinum they are more likely to resume exports of the former. In the markets for the other platinum group metals the biggest factor is demand. Their major uses, apart from in jewellery, are all highly technical which, as industry becomes more sophisticated, ensures a growing demand. The use of these metals will be limited not so much by price as by physical availability.

Part 2:
The monetary role of gold

The monetary role of gold

Tim Read

Gold has played a leading role in international monetary relations for at least 2500 years. Its history is inextricably tied to the rise and fall of great empires, for it has exerted greatest influence during periods of hegemony – whether that of Darius's Persia or Victoria's Britain.

The authority, which the metal has commanded for these two and a half millennia, has been derived from its intrinsic properties – namely its beauty, its permanence, its mass and, of course, its scarcity. It was revered by the ancient civilizations of Mesopotamia and Egypt and generally accepted as a store of value. It formed the basis for trade between the various parts of the Middle East and coins were issued by the Babylonians of a gold-silver alloy known as electrum. These, however, were subject to adulteration by the variation of the gold silver ratio, and so were not totally accepted.

The first standardized gold coinage was minted by the Kings of Lydia from about 650 BC. The gold came from Lydia's own mines in Anatolia. The economic power, which Lydia enjoyed as a consequence of its strong currency, reached its zenith under the last king, Croesus, who to this day is famed for his enormous wealth.

The Lydian monetary system was not a pure gold standard – rather it was bimetallic in that silver coins were also minted. However, a fixed relationship was determined between the two metals and a tight control was maintained over the supply of each. In such an economic climate gold became readily acceptable both as a medium of exchange and as a unit of account.

Lydia eventually succumbed to the superior military strength of Persia with the defeat of Croesus at Sardis. Its gold-based monetary system was, however, adopted and developed by the Persians who eventually came to control most of the civilized world's gold mining resources. When the Persians were in turn beaten by the armies of Alexander the Great, gold became the economic cornerstone of the Macedonian Empire. There occurred, during Alexander's reign, the first recorded inflation. As his conquests extended to the mining regions of Egypt, increased quantities of gold became available. Gold's value relative to other commodities declined – in other words, prices rose.

Gold continued to exert considerable influence after Alexander's death and the disintegration of his Empire. The rise of Carthage was largely due to its supply of gold from the mines of Spain. The Carthaginians, a mercantile race, used it to finance their trade routes to the Levant and to Western Europe.

Following the sack of Carthage in the Punic Wars, Spain and its gold mines became the possessions of Rome. The development of the Republic and subsequently the Empire was funded by these acquisitions. Unfortunately, the supply of precious metals was insufficient to meet the claims made upon it. In the latter years of the Roman Empire, succeeding rulers attempted to extend this gold by debasing it with copper and zinc. In so doing they set in train a series of catastrophic inflations which seriously undermined the authority of the state and contributed to its eventual collapse. The historian H A L Fisher wrote:

'Again, the steady depreciation of the currency during the third century (AD) was productive of manifold evils and of a violent remedial measure in the reign of Aurelian over which men fought and died in the streets of Rome. Yet no one put out a theory of currency or realized that bad money drives out good.'

Prior to Rome's eventual collapse, the hub of power had shifted to Constantinople. The Byzantine Emperors apparently had a much keener appreciation of monetary economics than their Roman forebears, because their gold-based currency, the solidus or byzant, lasted more or less intact until the twelfth century. It is no coincidence that for these 900 years of stable currency the power of the Byzantines was largely unassailed but in the twelfth century the Ottoman Turks began to threaten the Empire, the solidus was debased and inflation ensued.

During the Middle Ages, gold became increasingly accepted by the various Western European states as the ultimate store of value. England adopted a gold coinage in 1344 during the reign of Edward III. It was, however, a period of economic stagnation. No one country predominated – nearly every one was preoccupied with internal schism and civil war.

This stagnation was brought to an abrupt end with the discovery of the New World. The gold of Atahulpa and the silver of Montezuma were delivered into the hands of Spain which, on the proceeds, rapidly evolved into the most powerful nation in Europe. This flow of gold, in unprecedented quantities, led to a prolonged inflation throughout the continent. It was a precise repetition of the price explosion which had shaken Alexander's empire eighteen hundred years earlier.

Spain's rivals, England, France and Holland, perceived that there were close ties between the concentration of wealth and political power. They equated wealth with precious metals rather than with the merchandise that could be acquired in exchange for them. Thus evolved the principles of 'bullionism', by which the accumulation of gold and silver became a preoccupying political objective of the leading states.

This philosophy was succinctly stated by Monchretien, a French economist of the early seventeenth century:

'We live not so much from trade in raw materials as from gold and silver.'

Each nation pursued a policy of running a balance of payments surplus in order to amass reserves of metallic currency. The export of precious metals was generally proscribed : in Spain, it was an offence punishable by death. However, such a system could not be sustained without increasing Government control. The accumulation of reserves created an increase in domestic liquidity and this stimulated a demand for merchandise which could only be supplied by the expansion of domestic production, or by imports. In some respects it was an approach not totally dissimilar to twentieth century conditions. It was well appreciated that the maximization of reserves ensured fuller employment, providing that the domestic economy was protected by trade barriers. If there was no spare capacity in the economy, however, the inevitable result was demand inflation.

As stated gold's history is one of empires. The prominence which the metal achieved in the nineteenth century and the early part of the twentieth was bound up with the development of the British Empire and the burgeoning influence of the pound sterling. This was the age of the Gold Standard, a system totally opposed to the preceding mercantalist philosophies, since it was based upon classical 'laissez faire' economics.

Prior to the Industrial Revolution, England had maintained a bimetallic currency, with silver shillings co-existing with golden guineas. Progressively, however, gold gained the upper hand. Strict limits were placed upon the quantity of silver acceptable as legal tender and, in 1819, soon after the conclusion of the Napoleonic Wars, it was decided that paper currency could only be converted into gold.

Marcello de Cecco in his book *Money and Empire* defines the gold standard as follows:

'. . . a country is on a gold standard when gold is used as the ultimate numeraire of that country's monetary system, and/or when other means of payments in use there are readily redeemable in gold at their bearer's request.'

Britain maintained this position more or less in isolation from 1819 until 1871. The other European nations, which were less advanced industrially and consequently less aflluent, maintained bimetallic systems until much later in the century. The United States, too, was at first unwilling to adopt gold convertibility. Germany was the first nation to join Britain, in 1871. The United States followed two years later. In the next six years most of the other leading nations had abandoned silver and the supposed 'Golden Age' of the international Gold Standard had commenced. It was to last until the outbreak of war in 1914.

De Cecco further defines an international gold standard thus

'An international gold standard is said to exist when gold is the effective numeraire in most countries and/or when the other means of payment used as money/numeraire in those countries are readily redeemable in gold at their bearer's request.'

Let us examine how the international gold standard was expected to operate. In Britain, the unit account was the gold sovereign which contained 113.0016 grains of 24 carat gold. In the United States the dollar was convertible into 23.22 grains of fine gold. The exchange rate between the two currencies was, therefore, £1 equals $4.87. With the exchange rates fixed through the medium of gold, the monetary systems of the two countries became interdependent.

If Britain were to run a balance of payments deficit with the United States, this would be paid for by the shipment of an equivalent amount of gold or gold-convertible assets such as sterling. The Bank of England would replenish its reserves by selling gilt-edged securities to the commercial banks. This would have the effect of reducing domestic liquidity and of driving up interest rates. The results of such action were summarized by the Cunliffe Committee, reporting in 1929 on the operations of the Gold Standard, as follows:

'New enterprises were therefore postponed and the demand for construction materials and other capital goods lessened. The consequent slackening of employment also diminished the demand for consumable goods. And holders of stocks of commodities, carried largely with borrowed money, were confronted with an increase in interest charges, if not with actual difficulty in renewing loans, and with the prospect of falling prices tended to press their goods on a weak market. The result was a decline in general prices in the home market which, by checking imports and stimulating exports corrected the adverse trade balance which was the primary course of the difficulty.'

Conversely, the creditor country, in this case the United States, would have experienced a drop in interest rates, an expansion of credit and an inflation of domestic prices, which, in turn, would have rendered the country less competitive in export markets and more susceptible to imports. Hence the adjustment mechanism would nullify the surplus with the same efficiency that it attacked Britain's temporary deficit.

The success of the Gold Standard depended upon the willingness of every participating government to sacrifice all economic considerations to the primary objective of maintaining full convertibility. It assumed that each would adopt 'laissez faire' policies towards domestic prices, employment, economic growth etc, allowing these to be determined by the working of the adjustment process. Such were the 'rules of the game'. It is not difficult to appreciate the elements in this mechanism which many have found seductive. The symmetry with which it theoretically deals with surplus and deficit alike, the automatic nature of the adjustment, the minimization of the role of individual national governments in domestic economic policies, are all very positive qualities. Nostalgia for the system reached its high point in years following World War I, when contemporary economic chaos made the age of the Gold Standard appear the epitome of order and affluence. More recent examinations, however, have exposed the mythic nature of such views. They call into question whether the Gold Standard was ever allowed to operate with its theoretical freedom.

The two fundamental criticisms concern the role of national governments and the influence of long-term capital flows. Arthur Bloomfield, in his book *Monetary Policy Under the International Gold Standard, 1880-1913* demonstrated that the national governments were not as passive in their domestic economic policies as tradition would suggest. The so-called 'rules of the game' were often broken, as governments sought to neutralize the effects of the adjustment mechanism. It has been found that central banks indulged in open market operations to cancel out any effects of both gold outflows and inflows. That is to say when an export of gold reduced the liquidity base of an economy, instead of allowing this to drive up interest rates as the classical system would dictate, the central bank would neutralize the influence of this outflow by buying gilt-edged securities from the commercial banks, thus maintaining the level of the money supply.

That the balance of payments adjustment took place was due more probably to the influence of long-term capital flows. Robert Triffin in *Our International Monetary System: Yesterday Today and Tomorrow* points out:

'. . . international capital movements often did cushion – and even stimulate – vast and enduring deficits, or surpluses, on current account without calling for any correction whatsoever.'

This was a state of affairs far less symmetrical or even-handed than the classical model supposes. The wealthier nations amassed large portfolios of overseas investments and were able to liquidate them or add to them, rather than permit trade balances to affect domestic policies. Similarly, rapidly developing nations such as the United States, Canada and South Africa were able to expand their economies by utilizing inflows on Capital Account. London was the dominant capital market and its institutions were eager to make investments in the new mines, railways and industries of these countries.

The Gold Standard, as postulated in its classical form, did not exist. The system that persisted during this Golden Age was, in fact, a pound sterling standard. Britain was the most powerful nation throughout this period, although towards the close it was challenged by both Germany and the United States. The convertibility of the pound sterling partially disguised the inadequacy of Britain's gold reserves. The pound was regarded as being 'as good as gold', even though all foreign exchange reserves were held in gold. Britain took upon itself the role of lender to deficit countries, this, however, was not an act of altruism but one of enlightened self-interest because it kept markets open for British manufactures and investment.

The Gold Standard died with the declaration of war in August 1914. The militant nations, wishing to conserve their reserves, suspended convertibility and paper replaced gold as the medium of international exchange. When hostilities eventually ceased, the world economy was in a seriously debilitated condition. Britain had entered the war as the most powerful of nations – it was now considerably weaker owing vast amounts to the United States. It no longer could dictate the 'rules of the game'. Prices surged ahead throughout the war so that gold reserves, at their pre-war parities, were grossly inadequate to finance world trade. Yet there was no general agreement to revalue the price of gold. Furthermore, individual currencies had moved radically out of line with each other, creating other imbalances.

When the bastardized version of the Gold Standard was introduced in 1925, the results were catastrophic. It lasted for barely six years. The shortcomings of the pre-war system now became manifestly obvious. The inadequacy of reserves meant that countries with over-valued currencies were forced to pursue politically unacceptable deflationary policies. The rapid growth of trades unionism had made wages and prices much less flexible on the downside, which further exacerbated unemployment. Governments generally were less willing to pursue 'laissez-faire' policies when lengthening dole queues threatened political stability. Britain abandoned convertibility in 1931 and the United States two years later. The ensuing devaluation of the dollar by 41 percent pegged gold at $US35 per ounce, a price that was to be maintained for the next 37 years.

The inter-war years can be seen, with hindsight, as the period when the United States achieved economic dominance of the Western world. The failure of monetary relations during these two decades was probably due to its reluctance to assume the responsibilities that this position forced upon it. By the end of the Second World War, it had overcome these inhibitions. The formulation of a new spirit of international monetary co-operation which characterized the planning for the post-war reconstruction depended, to a considerable degree, upon the willingness of the United States to assume economic leadership.

The Bretton Woods Conference of 1944 established a modified version of the gold exchange standard which had prevailed for much of the inter-war period. Exchange rates were fixed at parities against gold which could only be varied if a currency was accepted as being fundamentally over- or under-valued. Gold and the convertible currencies were to act jointly as reserves. The system was strengthened by the formation of the International Monetary Fund – a pool of gold and foreign exchange able to be mobilized for the defence of any currency under pressure.

At the outset, the US dollar was the only major fully convertible currency. Furthermore the United States, in the immediate post-war period, exercised a considerable superiority over the ravaged European economies. Consequently the monetary system rapidly evolved into a dollar standard, with gold playing a relatively minor role. Gold was initially the main component of official reserves, however, supplies of new mined gold failed to keep pace with requirements for international liquidity. The fixed price of gold of $US35 per ounce acted as a serious deterrent to mining companies in looking for new mineral deposits. Operating and capital costs increased significantly over their pre-war levels and the rate of return available to the gold mining industry declined steadily from 1946 onwards.

As gold was unable to provide the liquidity necessary to finance the expansion of the world economy, it was vital that the dollar should do so. For the first 12 years of the new system's operation, liquidity was inadequate because the United States' balance of payments was not consistently in deficit. From 1958 onwards, however, a tacit understanding was reached whereby the United States was permitted to run up such deficits thus providing its trading partners with a constant inflow of dollars.

At first, this worked fairly well because the rate of inflation in the United States was generally lower than that of its major competitors. Furthermore, its economic strength was largely unassailed. This state of affairs should also be viewed in the context of America's military leadership of the West which necessitated heavy overseas defence expenditures. The bargain was generally regarded as a fair one.

Things started to go wrong during the middle sixties. The US rate of inflation began to accelerate and, for the first time, the value of the dollar was questioned. Furthermore America's deepening involvement in Vietnam was becoming unacceptable to many countries. There was a growing sense of unease that the rest of the world should be carrying the costs of America's inadequate domestic economic control and its overseas military adventures. In consequence an ever increasing quantity of dollars was offered for conversion into gold.

Meanwhile, non-monetary demand for gold had expanded to a point at which it exceeded new mined supplies. Upward pressure upon the official price of $US35 per ounce intensified. If the monetary system were to remain intact, the price had to be defended and this entailed additional supplies of the metal being made available. Thus, in 1965, the central banks formed the Gold Pool to provide a theoretically perfect elastic supply of metal at the official price. It proved a failure. Over the course of the next three years, some $US2.75 billion worth of gold was drained from official reserves into the private sector. It became increasingly evident that gold was fundamentally undervalued and that such sales would not prevent an inevitable adjustment in its price. The Gold Pool was abandoned in 1968 and replaced by a two tier gold market. The official price was maintained for transactions between banks, and a free market was established for non-monetary purchases. Although, at first, the free gold price fell to below the official parity, it soon climbed to a significant premium. The effects of this upon the international monetary system was intolerable. The greater the gap between the two prices, the more speculation increased, based upon the assumption that that there would eventually be a revaluation of the official price. The dollar, at least, in principle, was convertible at the official price so the outflow of US gold reserves accelerated. All new mined gold production was going to the free market, hence there was none available to increase liquidity. Lastly the disparity between the two prices prevented the central banks from utilizing their reserves as a means of international settlement. They had no wish to ship gold at what was so obviously an unrealistically low price. The situation was untenable and on 15 August 1971 the United States abandoned the dollar's convertibility and the gold exchange standard was dead.

Why did the Bretton Wood's system fail? The crumbling of the dollar's dominance was largely responsible. However, the role of gold was not blameless. There was a fatal inconsistency in a system which took gold as its basic numeraire, ie it required the gold price to be fixed; and yet ensured that there was a fundamental supply/demand imbalance for the metal, as a commodity, which in turn meant that its price had to rise. The increasing awareness of this situation added fuel to the fires of speculation.

The realization that gold was a destabilizing influence in world monetary affairs strengthened the resolve of the prominent economic powers to reduce its influence. Hence the period since 1971 has witnessed a progressive trend towards demonetization.

In 1968, the dollar and gold had been supplemented as reserve currencies by the Special Drawing Right. The SDR was, in effect, a credit note backed by the reserves of the IMF. Initially it was regarded as 'paper gold' because each unit carried a value equivalent to $\frac{1}{35}$ of a troy ounce of fine gold. Since 1971, the SDR has played an increasingly important role as a reserve asset. It was vital that it also assumed the function of numeraire. In order to achieve this, its links with gold had to be severed – so its value was redefined in terms of a basket of leading currencies. Gold ceased to have any relevance as unit of account: a state of affairs underscored, in 1976, by the abandonment of the official price.

Gold remains a reserve asset but, like any other commodity, its price is allowed to fluctuate with the pressures of the free market supply and

Table 1: Structure of International Monetary Reserves 1968[1] and 1978[2]

SDR Millions

		Gold	Foreign Exchange	SDR	IMF Reserve Positions	Total Reserves
Group of Ten + Switzerland	1968	31,000	17,177	–	5,162	53,339
		58.1%	32.2%	–	9.7%	100.0%
	1978(a)	29,166	104,013	5,682	8,829	147,690
		19.8%	70.4%	3.8%	6.0%	100.0%
	(b)	129,700	104,013	5,682	8,829	248,224
		52.2%	41.9%	2.3%	3.6%	100.0%
Other Developed Nations	1968	4,512	4,667	–	729	9,908
		45.5%	47.1%	–	7.4%	100.0%
	1978(a)	3,103	23,576	688	1,082	28,449
		10.9%	82.9%	2.4%	3.8%	100.0%
	(b)	13,799	23,576	688	1,082	39,145
		35.2%	60.2%	1.8%	2.8%	100.0%
Lesser Developed Nations	1968	2,123	7,869	–	431	10,423
		20.4%	75.5%	–	4.1%	100.0%
	1978(a)	1,942	46,699	1,178	814	50,633
		3.8%	92.2%	2.3%	1.7%	100.0%
	(b)	8,636	46,699	1,178	814	57,327
		15.0%	81.5%	2.1%	1.4%	100.0%
Oil Exporting Nations	1968	1,305	2,187	–	166	3,658
		35.7%	59.8%	–	4.5%	100.0%
	1978(a)	1,260	40,243	480	4,642	46,625
		2.7%	86.3%	1.0%	10.0%	100.0%
	(b)	5,630	40,243	480	4,642	50,968
		11.0%	79.0%	0.9%	9.1%	100.0%
World Total	1968	38,940	31,900	–	6,488	77,328
		50.4%	41.2%	–	8.4%	100.0%
	1978(a)	35,471	214,531	8,028	15,367	273,397
		13.0%	78.5%	2.9%	5.6%	100.0%
	(b)	157,739	214,531	8,028	15,367	395,665
		39.9%	54.2%	2.0%	3.9%	100.0%

(1) End December

(2) End November
1968 (a) Valued at 35 SDR per ounce
(b) Valued at 155.6 SDR per ounce
(equivalent to $200)

Source: IMF

demand. The central banks are no longer prevented from buying or selling the metal on the open market.

It continues to be used by central banks as collateral for international loans and cross guarantees such as that granted to Italy by West Germany. The abolition of the official price has also enabled monetary reserves of gold to be revalued at levels closer to the current free market price. Italy, for example, values its gold reserves at 85 percent of the average gold price over the 30 days preceding any revaluation. France, on the other hand, revalues semi-annually at the average of daily prices over the last three months of the previous semester.

It is inevitable that this role will become eroded with time. The growth of the world economy will have a two-fold effect. First the accompanying need for liquidity will be provided by SDRs and foreign exchange, so the proportion accounted for by gold will diminish. Second, the demand for gold for non-monetary purposes is increasing at a rate of three to four percent per annum, whilst supply is fairly static. This means that gold will be siphoned from official reserves into the private sector.

In Table 1, the present structure of world reserves is compared with that which existed at the end of 1968. The 1978 figures value gold at both the old official price of 35 SDR's and at the then current free market price of $US200 per ounce. Even on this latter basis, the proportion of reserves held in the form of bullion has declined world-wide from 50.4 percent in 1968 to 39.9 percent in 1978. The 35 SDR valuation shows that over the 10-year period there has been a net physical diminution in the stocks of gold held – in total a drop of 3,082 tonnes from 34,604 tonnes to 31,522 tonnes. (One tonne is equivalent to 1.125 million SDR's at the official price).

In 1976, the IMF instituted a four-year programme of gold auctions which will, on completion, have reduced its metal reserves by 25 million ounces equivalent to 17 percent. A similar amount is being sold back to the contributing member nations at the former official price of 35 SDRs per ounce.

The divorce of gold from the monetary system has not been universally acclaimed. A significant body of opinion wishes to see this process thrown into reverse with a return to the classical gold standard. A system of fixed rates, with national governments committed to their maintenance, and gold as the sole reserve asset, would, it is argued, permit a return to monetary discipline. Running throughout this philosophy is an abhorrence of inflation and a profound disrespect for the ability of any national government to prevent it. If the money supply is determined by the level of international reserves, inflation can be controlled more effectively than by any government-operated fiscal or monetary policy. The gold lobby has one of its most eloquent spokesmen in William Rees Mogg. In a review of R W Jastram's *The Golden*

Constant, in *The Times,* 14 July 1978. Mogg concludes thus:

'The paper systems seem now to be coming to the end of their effective lives; the restoration of gold to a central position in world money is the most valuable reform that could be undertaken.

'The historic evidence is that gold is greatly more efficient than paper in producing stable prices and stable and low interest rates. These are the optimum monetary conditions for economic development and social stability. Gold has in the past provided a guarantee for centuries against world inflation; it would do so again.'

The philosophy is both economically and politically naive. As discussed earlier, the Gold Standard, in its heyday before 1914, did not work automatically: governments attempted to neutralize the harsher effects of the system's operation. This happened when 'laissez faire' economics was a universally accepted philosophy. It is unlikely that today's national governments, used as they are to much greater levels of state participation, would meekly hand over all economic authority to an unproven automatic mechanism. A democratic government, faced with the need to assuage its electorate, would succumb to the temptation of influencing the domestic money supply, thereby dampening those inflationary and deflationary gyrations which would characterize the adoption of such a standard.

Once the automatic nature of the system is lost, it ceases to work efficiently. Individual governments can completely isolate the effects of any changes in reserves upon the money supply. Another major problem is the lack of price symmetry in our modern world. The growing influence of trades unions has inhibited any significant falls in money wages during periods of recession. If wages do not fall in line with the money supply, unemployment will get worse.

The expanding non-monetary demand for gold presents another serious difficulty. New mined supply is the only source of additional liquidity – if it is fully absorbed outside the monetary system then the system cannot grow. The only means of providing liquidity in such circumstances would be a revaluation of gold against all currencies. This solution is highly unsatisfactory because it results in sudden inflationary jumps in liquidity and furthermore stimulates considerable speculation. If gold is revalued once, then it can be again.

The most clear-headed and pragmatic contributions to the subject of gold's monetary role during the past 10 years have come from the pen of Xenophon Zolotas, the former Governor of the Bank of Greece. He has consistently identified both the problems which the metal presents to the international financial community, and the measures needed to overcome them. Writing in 1974, Zolotas affirmed:

'It would indeed be a blunder to anchor again the international monetary system to such an erratically moving anchorage as gold.'

Recent history lends considerable support to the wisdom of this view. The past 15 years have witnessed the divorce of gold's twin monetary roles of store value and unit of account. The considerable faith that individuals and institutions hold in gold as a store of value appears unshakeable as evidenced by the recent rapid increase in price. However, this function depends upon its interacting as a commodity governed by the basic economic laws of supply and demand. After all, when the price of gold was held at $35 per ounce by international regulation, its value in real terms suffered a serious decline. It is as a unit of account at the hub of the monetary system – the numeraire against which all currencies are defined – that gold has probably ceased to have an active role.

Part 3:
Gold

Gold

Gold production: world total, 1968-1977
metric tons

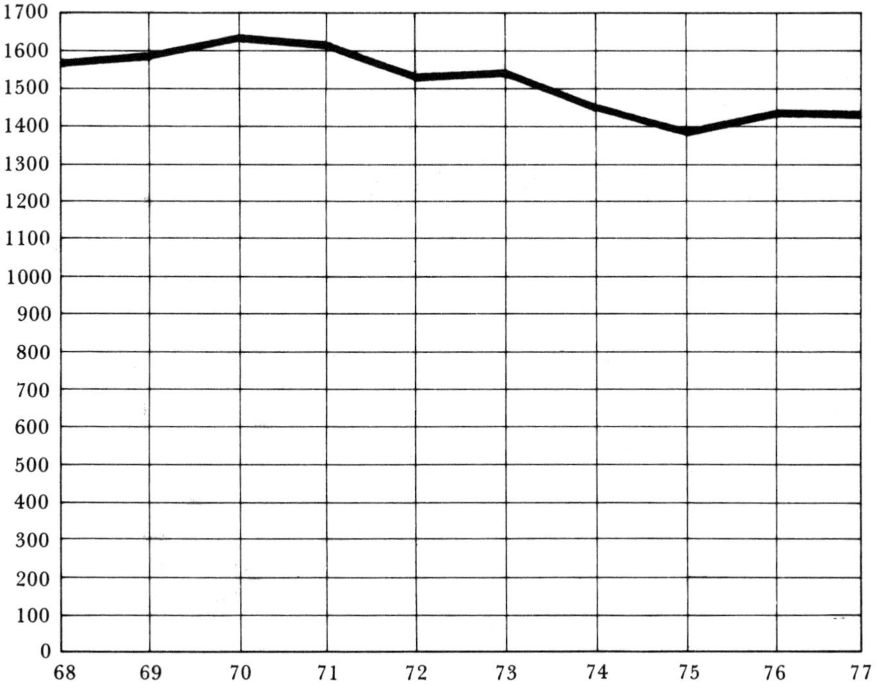

See Appendix 1, page 121

Source: Metal Bulletin

Grades available

Gold is traded internationally in troy ounces. For jewellery, and other decorative uses, the carat system is used to measure purity: in this system 24 carat gold is 100 per cent gold and therefore, for example, 12 carat is 50 per cent gold and 9 carat 9/24ths pure gold.

The colour of gold articles depends on the metal with which it is debased.

Gold production by country, 1977 *metric tons*

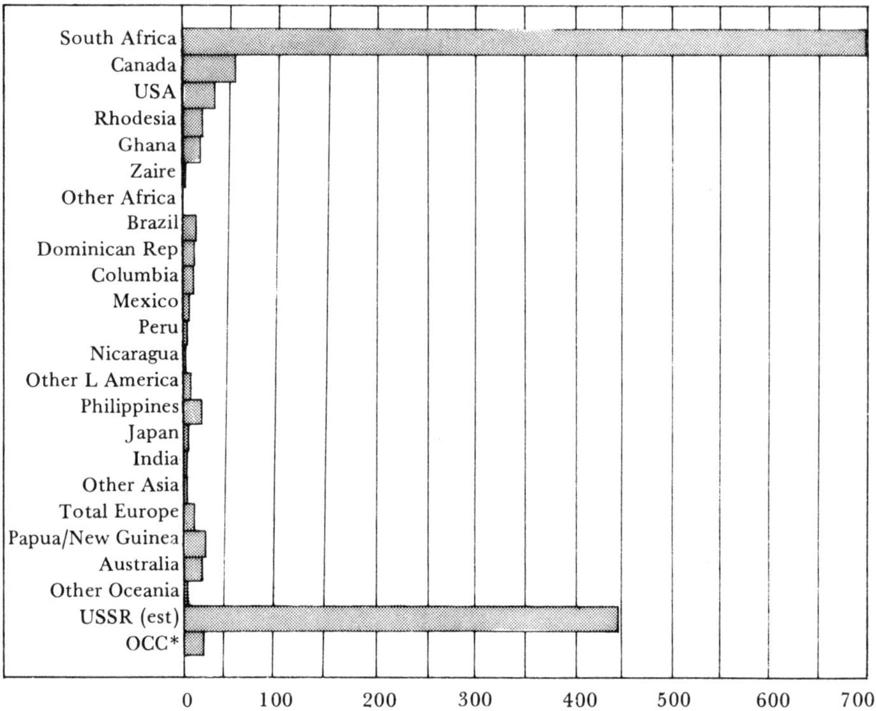

* Other communist countries *Source: Consolidated Goldfields*

See Appendix 1, pages 121, 122

Trade between dealers, banks and countries is usually conducted in gold bars with weights of 12.5 kilograms and a purity of 99.5 percent minimum.

In countries where the population is legally entitled to buy and sell gold, dealers often offer small ingots of a few ounces each.

Production method

As gold is almost incorruptible in natural circumstances, it is found in the earth in metallic form. In most deposits, however, it is so finely distributed that only a fraction of an ounce may be recoverable from the treatment of a tonne of ore. The gold may be finely dispersed in the ore of base metals from which it is produced as a by-product.

In some regions gold-containing ores have been weathered and the minerals surrounding the gold have been washed and blown away. In such areas gold may be found in nuggets or as dust deposits in streams and rivers.

A high proportion of the gold in most ores can be recovered by crushing and flotation or by gravity separation. The remaining untreated ore is either smelted by conventional means and/or treated with cyanide, then recovered as a precipitate from the solution by the addition of zinc dust.

Major uses

The demand/supply forces in the gold market are highly technical because of gold's role as a medium of exchange. It has a widespread use in jewellery and objets d'art owing partly to its unique physical properties and partly to its interchangeability with money. These decorative uses account for about 60 percent of demand. In order to facilitate the mechanical processes of turning the metal into robust articles it must, almost invariably, be alloyed with other metals, particularly copper, zinc, silver and nickel.

Gold has several other important commercial uses. In electronics it is used in wiring; combined with silicon and/or other metals it is made into tiny chips and used for certain semi-conductors as contacts and in printed circuits. Dentists are responsible for about 12 percent of gold consumption, for artificial teeth, caps and fillings. It has several other minor uses in the chemical industry and in medicine, especially in applications where resistance to corrosion is important.

Gold consumption (worldwide) by uses, 1976

End Use	*metric tons*
Jewellery	885
Electronics	72
Dentistry	69
Other industrial (decorative)	78
Official coins	180
Medals, medallions and fake coins	22
	1306

Total production 1415 metric tons

Balance between consumption and production explained by the following factors, 1976

Increase in central bank holdings	14
Increase (decrease) in IMF holdings	(121)
Communist bloc production not reaching West	140
Increase (decrease) in hoarding of bars	–
Increase (decrease) in private speculative and investment holdings	76
	1415

Source: Johnson Matthey Bankers Ltd, estimates from Consolidated Goldfields chart

Gold: consumption, 1977 (excluding USSR) *metric tons*

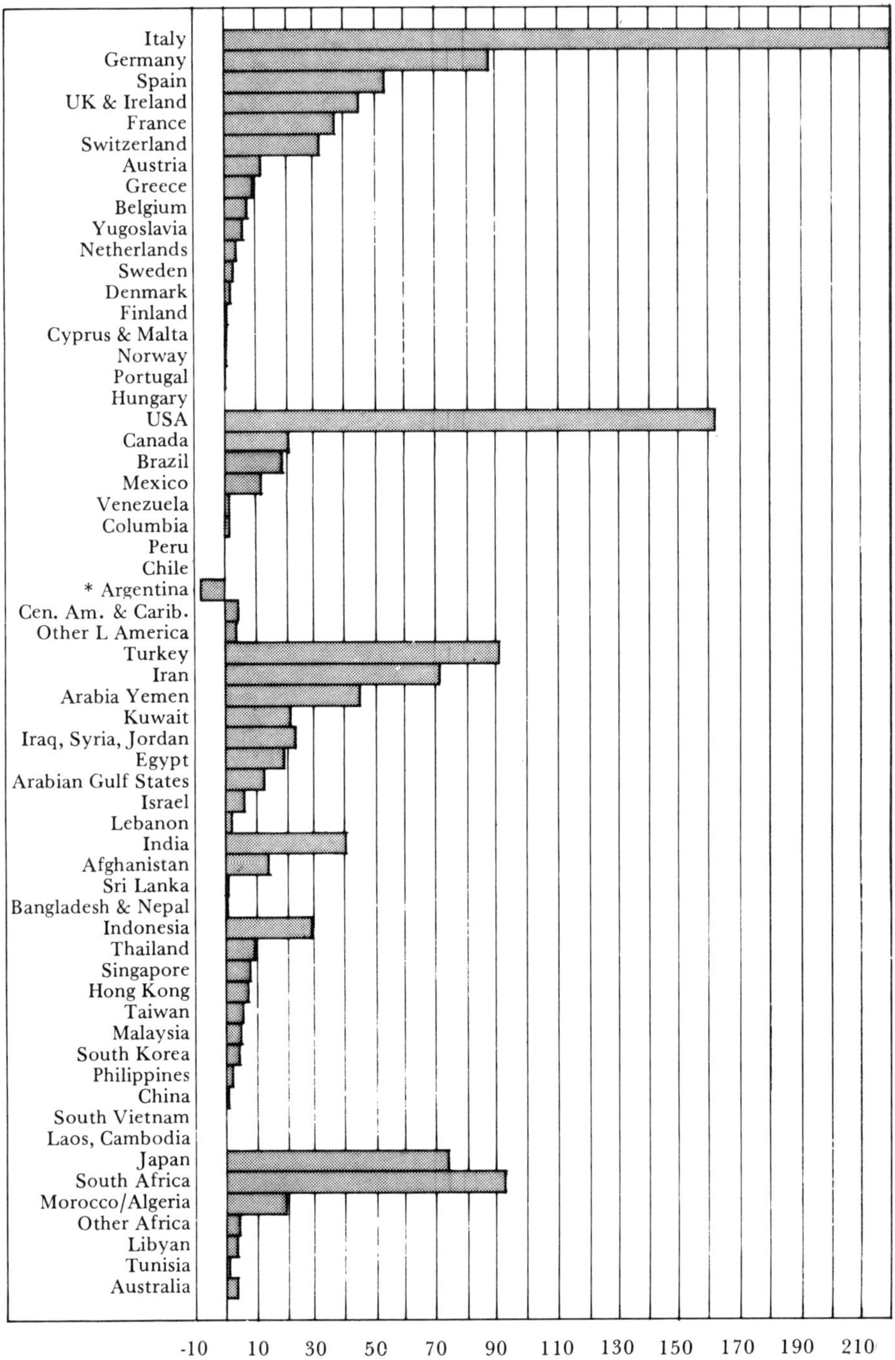

Total excluding the USSR 1386.9 metric tons *Source: Consolidated Goldfields*

**Negative consumption is due to the dishoarding of gold in consequence of the political climate.*
See Appendix 1, pages 127, 128

Main market features

When, in the late 1960's it became clear that the US Government was incapable of keeping the gold price as low as $35, most experts predicted that the price would double in the 1970s. This forecast was, of course, far too conservative and did not make the correct assumptions in two important areas.

First, the ability of gold consumers, especially in the jewellery trade, to pay higher prices. This error is understandable since no data was available as to the impact of price movements on demand. Gold was one of the very few commodities that had not changed in price for the previous 30 years.

Second, the rise in world inflation, caused in part by the massive increase in the price of oil, was difficult to predict. High inflation rates indirectly caused instability in the most important currencies and this encouraged investment in gold. Investment in gold does not need to be a perfect hedge against the fall of a currency's value, people have only to believe that it is.

The main difficulty in making predictions concerning gold price levels is that, unlike most commodities, gold has the distinction of being partly a commodity, partly money, and partly decorative, as in jewellery.

When viewed as an industrial commodity, gold is a poor sort of investment. Only about 17 percent of gold supplies are used in electronics and other industrial uses.

The reasons for the current demand for gold are: that it is rare, although many metals are rarer; it is expensive to produce, although again several metals have a higher cost of production; it is attractive; it takes up little storage room; it is easy to fabricate into jewellery; it does not deteriorate with age; it is very resistant to corrosion, although in a pure state it is rather soft and by no means resistant to wear; and that it is, by convention and tradition, a substitute for money and has a good record for keeping its value in critical economic situations.

This last fact more than any other is the one that sets it apart from other metals or commodities. Unfortunately, it is also this fact that is the most difficult to quantify in terms of demand. A better investment proposition would surely be a commodity that people could actually use, such as the metals used in industry, or fuels which must be used to produce almost everything, or a direct investment in industry which is bound to be encouraged by any government. The demand for gold is at root based upon convention and one must therefore expect price fluctuations and the possibility, however slight, of a loss of confidence in the intrinsic value of this metal.

With high inflation, a comparatively poor performance by the bulk of industry in the West, unstable currencies and political unrest, and with no clear end to these problems in sight, most people still view gold as a sensible investment. It is therefore reasonable to study the day-to-day influences on the gold price.

Unlike many other investments, it is difficult to derive an income from purchasing gold except by selling options, which has its own dangers and difficulties. However, although tax laws are different in all countries, a gain made by buying and selling gold is usually not penalized as much as income gained in the form of dividends or in similar ways.

Price rises in gold often coincide with periods of tightening credit and rising interest rates and these, in turn, coincide with low industrial performance, balance of payments problems and other such depressions in the economy. Unfortunately it is in just such periods that governments, the IMF and other gold-stocking bodies find it necessary to sell quantities of gold. Careful consideration of all potential gold sales on the market must be made by the short-term investor, as sales from sources other than mined production can be a high proportion of total supplies available to the market. In 1967, for instance, sales from these sources actually exceeded gold production in the Western world.

Figures describing demand for gold for industrial uses, jewellery and coins can be obtained from stockbrokers, banks and precious metal merchants and are essential information.

The cost of producing gold is certain to continue increasing. Gold production is costly in both labour and capital and the shortage of skilled labour, especially in South Africa, must mean higher labour costs. With the disruption of oil supplies from Iran to South Africa, internal oil prices are expected to rise substantially with a consequent rise in the rate of inflation. Although the cost of fuel is not a high factor in gold production increased inflation will have a considerable indirect effect.

The prospect of long-term oil shortages in South Africa is likely to accelerate the development of nuclear power in the country. This will mean increased production of uranium, much of which is produced with gold as a by-product, therefore a small increase of gold production can be expected. However, production costs for any commodity are never as important as demand factors and with vast and growing oil revenues in the Middle East, consumption in the form of jewellery has increased to the point where almost one-third of all gold jewellery production is purchased by those countries. This trend is expected to continue.

The uses of gold in industry are mainly confined to electronics. Although this industry is booming, it will not produce any dramatic increase in gold consumption because the trend is to miniaturize electronic systems. In addition, efforts are being made to find substitutes for gold because of its high cost.

South Africa represents the largest source of new supplies but production there has been falling in spite of increasing prices. It seems that South African gold mining policy is to refine low grade gold ores when prices are high and high grade ores when prices are low. This policy makes sense, as extracting gold from low grade ores is a more expensive operation. If, in addition, the South Africans were to limit gold production this would ensure a healthy balance between producing too much, which might lower gold prices, and producing too little, which would not provide enough income.

In 1978 the Soviet Union all but ceased making gold available to the Western market, which has further tightened the supply. South African production is unlikely to compensate for this loss for the reasons stated above and most observers agree that the Soviet Union has no great need, in the near future, to earn foreign currency by the sale of large quantities of gold, especially as their gold mines are more expensive to run than those in South Africa.

Since 1975 the American public have been free to buy and sell gold as individuals. This has meant a great boom for the companies who market small ingots and coins. These years have coincided with a period of recession and a falling dollar, which is the first experience most Americans have had of such problems. Gold buying has been spurred by fears of hyper-inflation or a slump on the scale of 1929 and by the fact that such buying has been profitable in the past.

People in Germany or Switzerland who bought gold have not done so well. Gold, in terms of their currencies, has not increased as much. But many holders of dollars outside the United States have been tempted to exchange their dollars for gold and may continue to do so if they think that the dollar will weaken further.

Although gold is officially demonetized in most industrial countries, it is still the policy of many countries, notably those in the EEC, to have a proportion of their currency backed by gold reserves. The situation thus remains confused.

The case for gold is that it keeps its value during periods of world recession and is a useful hedge for natives of a country where the currency is falling in value, compared with that of other currencies.

However, in a prolonged period of recession holders of gold who are in a weak financial position may have to sell to sustain themselves; and governments are likely to discourage gold hoarding if they think that investment in gold is depleting the pool of investment available to industry. Furthermore, when a recessionary period comes to an end, people will overcome their fears, be encouraged to make less sterile investments and want to sell their gold to invest in something more useful. After all, you can't eat gold.

Methods of trading

There have been radical changes in the marketing of gold since price control was effectively removed in the late 1960s. Markets selling gold, either for immediate delivery, or for delivery at some future date, have been set up throughout the world to reflect the constant price fluctuations and to disseminate gold buying to a much wider public, as restrictions have been relaxed. Britain is now one of the few industrialized countries in the world where private citizens are still not allowed to buy gold (except for Krugerrands and jewellery) for speculative or investment purposes: purchases can be made only by authorized companies and banks, either for industrial use and jewellery manufacture or for trading internationally.

In the rest of the world, however, the demand for gold has been increasing from private investors seeking to protect their funds against inflation and against currency changes that have undermined the value of paper money.

The flow of gold onto world markets naturally starts from the main producing areas – South Africa and the Soviet Union. Until the 1960s when the price of gold was held at the artificial level of $35 an ounce, the bulk of South Africa's production was shipped by the Union Castle to the Bank of England in London, which acted as a marketing agent throughout the rest of the world. However, with the expulsion of South Africa from the British Commonwealth and the breaking of traditional links between the two countries, South Africa decided to take over its own gold marketing and diverted most of its shipments for sale via the Swiss banks in Zurich.

The South African Chamber of Mines also stepped up production of Krugerrands, the coins equivalent to an ounce of gold, but sold by producers at a more profitable rate to a much wider clientele able to buy only small quantities. The South African Government through its Central Bank keeps a strict control over the sale of newly-mined gold. But there are vast quantities of gold stocks that change hands between the various marketing and distribution centres throughout the world. Supplies from the Soviet Union – the world's second biggest producer of gold – and the many other producers throughout the world come onto the markets in various ways, either under supply contracts with consumers, or via merchants and brokers. Despite the loss of its traditional links with South Africa, London still vies with Zurich, the United States and Far Eastern countries as an important gold trading centre.

Five bullion brokers, with considerable knowledge and expertise built up over the years, dominate the London gold market. They meet twice a day – once in the morning and once in the afternoon – for the official 'fixing' of prices. The actual fixing is surrounded by secrecy, with outsiders excluded but it is relatively simple. The five brokers assess their current purchases and sales, and decide at what price they would be prepared to do business with each other. What emerges, after some haggling, is the fixing – the price agreed at a particular point. In fact trading goes on all day, both before, during and after the fixings, but some kind of official prices are required as the basis of contracts between buyers and sellers. Many suppliers, selling gold for delivery at some future date, will base the price charged either on the current fixing or the fixing on the day of delivery. Although fixing is held in London – at the offices of NM Rothschild, one of the five bullion brokers – it reflects trading conditions throughout the world since the majority of deals done by the bullion brokers are international, rather than confined to Britain. In addition to N M Rothschild, the bullion brokers are Johnson Matthey, Sharps Pixley, Mocatta and Goldsmid and Samuel Montagu. All have strong connections with the banking community, although Johnson Matthey are also important refiners of gold for industrial purposes and for jewellery. In 1978 Derby and Company were authorized to deal in gold but have not yet joined the other brokers in the fixing.

Leading Swiss banks control the Zurich market, which usually has a major influence on the London fixing. At the same time sales of gold are handled by banks throughout the world. They sell physical supplies of gold either for industrial use or to trade and private speculators for investment. The shift in the world economy as a result of the flow of money to the oil producing countries and other emerging areas has resulted in the growth of important new markets in Hong Kong and, in 1978, in Singapore. Trading in gold is widespread and no longer controlled by the banking community. It is a commodity, not as firmly tied to the monetary system as it was before, and subject to supply and demand fluctuations in its own right. The main influences remain financial, rather than industrial. Buying and selling in this new unrestricted free market is controlled neither by central banks nor by governments, as it was in the past.

Futures markets are used as a protection against unpredictable fluctuations in the price of gold. Indeed the basic function of a futures market is to provide protection against losses in the physical transaction of a commodity by entering into an opposite transaction in 'paper' futures. The two balance each other out, whatever happens to the price. Futures are not supposed to be centres for physical trading, they are designed for paper transactions that are cancelled out before the delivery date falls due. But they do play an important part in influencing prices, since they reflect the price buyers are prepared to pay at a date in the future and also take in the many diverse influences at work. These markets have grown enormously in importance since the United States lifted its ban on private trading in gold in 1975. The immediate reaction was to launch a series of gold futures markets on the existing

United States commodity futures exchanges in Chicago and New York. After a slow start, at the time when the United States Government persuaded the public that gold was not a good investment, the futures markets took off after the value of the dollar started to fall and inflation became a serious threat. The two leading gold futures markets to emerge in the United States were COMEX (Commodity Exchange, Inc) and on the Chicago Mercantile Exchange. Other markets, including one on the Chicago Board of Trade, have not succeeded to the same extent. A considerable flow of funds goes into gold futures trading; rising and falling according to the general attitude towards the economy, supply/demand projections and the feeling among investors as to whether gold is over- or under-valued at a particular time.

The volume of funds coming into the futures markets, and the publication each day of prices arrived at in open-outcry trading, as opposed to the secretive London fixing, means that futures are having an increasingly important effect on world prices. Prices on international markets rapidly line up with each other unless there are exceptional circumstances as a result of traders operating worldwide, using the differences between the markets to make profits. If gold is cheaper in New York than it is in Zurich, traders will buy in New York thus pushing prices up, and sell at a profit in Zurich thus pushing prices down, until the two markets come into line and it is no longer profitable to trade. This arbitrage trading can be carried on throughout the world, taking into account the different influences at work in individual markets.

Futures markets are not confined to the United States. A forerunner of the United States markets was established in Winnipeg, Canada, which, in 1979, became the first market trading gold options. Increasingly important gold futures markets have been established in Hong Kong, Sydney and Singapore. The renewed popularity of gold, following the collapse of the world's two reserve currencies and the failure of Special Drawing Rights (SDRs) to provide an alternative standard, suggests that the futures markets will become an established part of the world marketing of gold. Thus, while the physical trading is likely to remain in the hands of the producers, industrial consumers, merchants and the banking community, influence on pricing will be exercised by the many trade and private investors participating via the paper futures markets.

The Gold Market in South Africa

South Africa's gold mines all refine their metal at the Rand Refinery in Germiston. The metal is delivered to the refinery in the form of bars containing about 88 percent gold, 10 percent silver and two percent base metal.

Although the refinery is operated by the South African Chamber of

Mines, the shares in it are owned by the mines themselves, in proportion to the contributions made over the previous year. The refined gold is sold to the Reserve Bank, which credits the mines directly.

The refinery casts the gold into 12.5 kilo bars with a purity of 99.5 percent. Some of this gold is purified further to 99.9 percent for industrial use.

The gold used to make Krugerrands is debased with copper from 99.9 percent to a purity of 91.66 percent, ie 22 carat gold. Krugerrands are struck by the South African Mint and some 150,000 are produced each week.

Gold coins

Like gold shares, coin prices are only partially affected by gold bullion prices. The other factors affecting value vary in relation to the coin under consideration.

Gold content

A buyer should know the purity of the coins he intends to purchase. Krugerrands and golden sovereigns are $\frac{916\ 2/3}{1000}$, ie $\frac{22}{24}$ or 22 carat. Copper is the metal normally used to debase the gold to this level.

Weight

The important factor is the weight of gold contained in the coin, ie a Krugerrand weighs 33.19 grams but contains 1 troy ounce or 31.1 grams of gold.

Other coins have a varying gold content. American coins usually contain 90 percent gold and have a higher weight to gold weight ratio.

Numismatic value

Among the most popular gold coins, eg Krugerrands, sovereigns and double eagles, there are some that are of particular interest because of a rare date or other unusual factors. However, it is unlikely that one of these coins would be included in a purchase from a bank or broker. Rare Krugerrands and sovereigns could be worth a high premium over the price of those with common dates but such premiums would, of course, be subject to a different market created by coin collectors.

Condition

Gold is a soft metal and coins can be easily marked or scored. Buyers need to take great care that coins are packed in such a way as to prevent them rubbing together. A coin may lose all its premium over the gold price if it has what is known as a 'bag mark', ie a scratch. Containers which keep coins unmarked are available from coin dealers.

Government taxes and regulations

The laws controlling coin deals are a most important factor affecting the premium a coin may have, over the value of the gold it contains.

Some governments, including that of the United Kingdom, make a distinction between coins which are legal tender in the country of origin, ie Krugerrands, and those which are not – the difference is that value added tax is chargeable on those coins which are not legal tender.

Governments may discourage speculation in gold coins for either economic or political reasons by restricting imports.

The last British Government (1974-1979) banned imports of all new gold coins, except by registered dealers. These could only be bought by non-residents or from external funds. This created a two-tier market in the United Kingdom, especially for Krugerrands and sovereigns where, for residents (who could only buy coins imported before these restrictions were implemented) the premium above the gold price was higher than that paid by non-residents who pay with external funds. The new Conservative Government has removed this restriction. Other governments make gold coins subject to sales tax. The price of the same coin therefore can vary from country to country.

Premiums

Most gold-containing coins are worth more than the gold they contain but the premium varies with the supply of, and demand for, the coins. There are no easy rules relating the change in premium to the movement of the gold price itself. The premium may increase when the price of gold is either going up or coming down; it depends on the market for the coin at the time. The investor would be wise to check the average premium for a particular coin over an extended period and to take this into consideration when timing the purchase.

It is possible to make money by buying and selling coins without the gold price changing at all, or to make a bigger profit than would be made by buying or selling the same quantity of pure gold. Similarly, it is possible to lose money in spite of a rise in the gold price. This could occur because of a fall in the premium; the difference between the coin dealer's buying and selling price; or a combination of both.

Investors interested in gold often have to trade coins as they are not allowed to deal in the pure metal ingots, nor do they want to take the additional risks associated with gold shares. In other words, coins are their only access to the gold market. As the gold price is by far the biggest influence on coin prices it is reasonable, for those who wish to buy gold, to buy it in coin form. It is important, however, to be aware of the other factors affecting values.

Gold coins are produced by governments to make more money than they would by selling the metal in ingot form. If too many are minted, demand will become saturated and the premium over the gold price will disappear. If this happened it would not pay the government to undertake the expense of minting them.

Gold coins, even those which are supposed to be legal tender, are not made of base metal, like other coinage. They have value by virtue of their gold content combined with their rarity. There is, therefore, no danger of gold-producing countries, or any other country producing a large amount of gold coinage which would have the effect of drastically reducing the premium. However, it is a well-known fact that, in a falling market small investors, who can least afford a loss tend to 'panic sell' and, as gold coins have become a popular speculation for small investors over the last decade, the prospect of a large fall in the price of gold may precipitate such heavy selling of coins that the premium does disappear.

Anyone contemplating a very large deal in gold coins – of some 1,000 ounces or more – should consider the effect that such a deal would have on the market. It would depend on the type of coin to be traded, the country, and the time in which it is to be traded. A purchase of, around, 2,000 Krugerrands, bought on a quiet day on the internal London market, may increase the premium by two or three percent.

Gold coins glossary

Bullion:	Precious metal ingots.
Face Value:	(Also nominal value). Value fixed by country of origin for use as legal tender.
Gross Weight:	The weight of a coin.
Fine Weight:	The weight of gold contained in a coin, determined by multiplying the gross weight by the fineness.
Fineness:	Measure of gold purity, measured in carats or as parts per thousand. Twenty-four carat gold is pure gold, ie 24/24 or 1000/1000 fineness known as fine gold. Eighteen carat is thus 18/24 pure gold or 750/1000 fineness.
Lator:	Gold coins of the former Latin Monetary Union. Term used mainly for Italian or Belgian coins of nominal value 20 lira or 20 Belgian francs.
Mint Mark:	Mark often too small to read on coin which identifies mint at which it was struck.

Popular gold coins

Krugerrand – South Africa
1 troy ounce fine gold
33.1903 grams, 916 $\frac{2}{3}$/1000
31mm diameter

Sovereign – Great Britain
7.9881 grams, 916 $\frac{2}{3}$/1000 fine gold
22mm diameter

Half sovereign – Great Britain
3.9940 grams, 916 $\frac{2}{3}$/1000 fine gold
19mm diameter

Double Eagle – United States
20 dollar gold piece
33.4370 grams, 900/1000 fine gold
34mm diameter

Eagle – United States
10 dollar gold piece
16.7185 grams, 900/1000 fine gold
27mm diameter

Ducat – Austria
3.4909 grams, 986 $\frac{2}{3}$/1000 fine gold
20mm diameter

Sovrano – Austria
11.060 grams, 919/1000 fine gold
28.5mm diameter

50 Pesos piece – Mexico
41.6666 grams, 900/1000 fine gold
37mm diameter

20 Pesos piece – Mexico
16.6666 grams, 900/1000 fine gold
27mm diameter

10 Pesos piece – Mexico
8.3333 grams, 900/1000 fine gold
22mm diameter

100 Schillings – Austria
23.5240 grams, 900/1000 fine gold
33mm diameter

10 Soles – Peru
4.68 grams, 900/1000 fine gold
18mm diameter

Vreneli (or 20 Francs) – Switzerland
6.4516 grams, 900/1000 fine gold
21mm diameter

10 Francs – Swizterland
3.2258 grams, 900/1000 fine gold
19mm diameter

Chervonetz – Soviet Union
8.6026 grams, 900/1000 fine gold
22.5mm diameter

20 Francs – France
Known as Napoleon
6.4516 grams, 900/1000 fine gold
21mm diameter

20 dollars – Canada
18.2733 grams, 900/1000 fine gold
27mm diameter

20 Francs – Belgium
Known as Lator
6.4516 grams, 900/1000 fine gold
21mm diameter

20 Lira – Italy
Also known as Lator
6.4516 grams, 900/1000 fine gold
21mm diameter

Gold Shares

The equity financing of the major gold discoveries during both the last century and the present one has led to an extensive global market in gold shares. For some years the South African mines have formed by far the largest component of this market, although there are a number of mines with public share quotations domiciled in Canada, Australia, the United States and the Philippines.

Gold mining shares offer an alternative medium for investment to bullion and coins, having one substantial advantage over the metal itself. If profitable a mine may pay a dividend giving an income yield on the investment whereas, with storage and insurance costs, the metal may have a small negative yield. This dividend yield on the shares can be a significant factor: at present many of the South African stocks are offering a 20 percent return on their current prices quite apart from capital appreciation considerations. However, it must be remembered that a mine is an investment with a finite life. It can only generate an income as long as there is ore which can be extracted profitably. Once this ore reserve is exhausted, the mine is worth only its break-up value, which may be minimal. Consequently the original cost of the investment must be recouped through the dividend income. Bullion and coins, on the other hand, will have a market value at the termination of the investment.

The high income available on the shares reflect the greater diversity of risk to which they are subject. An investment in gold is subject specifically to the market risk of the metal price. The price of gold shares too will be largely determined by this factor, in addition it will be subject to political, economic and technical risks.

The political risks extend beyond the internal stability of the country in which the mines are located, although this can be of crucial importance to the level of share prices as evidenced by the Sharpeville and Soweto riots in South Africa. Changes in royalty and tax rates, the stiffening of environmental regulations, and the dangers of asset sequestration will have considerable influence. The profitability of the mines will be affected not only by the gold price but also by the level of operating costs which, in turn, will be determined by the inflation rates of the major factors of production namely labour, fuel, spares and stores. The technical risks of investment in gold mining are numerous. These include changes in ore grade, the imperfect knowledge of ore reserves which means uncertainty regarding mine life, and natural disasters such as floodings and subsidence.

An important consideration to be taken into account is that once gold prices improve, it is standard practice for the mines, and the stated policy of the South African mining authorities, to increase ore reserves to include all hitherto unprofitable material which can now be mined at a profit. It is further required that the mines excavate ore averaging the same grade as that of the ore reserves of the mine as a whole. The intention of these requirements is to ensure that all profitable ore is extracted. This, however, results in the grade falling when the gold price rises which naturally trims profit margins.

In general the price of gold shares will move in line with the metal price although, at a more highly leveraged rate, in both directions. There will also be occasions when one or other may lag. Over the year to September 1979, gold bullion in sterling terms gave a return, before tax, of 42 percent whilst gold shares, including both capital appreciation and dividends, returned 59 percent.

South African Gold shares

Company	A	B	C	D	E	F	G
Blyvoors	4.93	71.4	89.5	102.0	14.5	18.2	20.7
Bracken	1.12	43.0	45.2	50.3	38.4	40.4	44.9
Buffelsfontein	13.00	195.5	206.1	241.3	15.0	15.9	18.6
Deelkraal	1.78	–	–	–	–	–	–
Doornfontein	3.85	48.9	105.6	125.7	12.7	27.4	32.6
East Driefontein	10.50	112.4	125.7	140.7	10.7	12.0	13.4
Elandsrand	4.70	–	–	–	–	–	–
Ergo	4.00	–	60.3	70.4	–	15.1	17.6
F.S. Geduld	23.44	307.9	361.9	417.2	13.1	15.4	17.8
F.S. Saaiplaas	1.12	–	–	–	–	–	–
Grootvlei	1.71	37.1	45.2	53.3	21.7	26.4	31.2
Harmony	4.23	65.5	115.6	138.2	15.5	27.3	32.7
Hartebeestfontein	18.94	278.6	306.6	346.8	14.7	16.2	18.3
Kloof	10.00	53.8	115.6	150.8	5.4	11.6	15.1
Kinross	4.02	53.8	70.4	77.4	13.4	17.5	19.3
Leslie	0.79	20.5	27.1	31.7	25.9	34.3	40.1
Libanon	8.40	107.5	155.8	178.4	12.8	18.5	21.2
Loraine	1.00	–	–	5.0	–	–	5.0
P. Brand	14.06	146.6	286.5	319.2	10.4	20.4	22.7
P. Steyn	11.06	78.2	175.9	206.1	7.1	15.9	18.6
Randfontein	44.88	439.9	854.5	1005.3	9.8	19.0	22.4
St. Helena	12.63	185.7	231.2	263.9	14.7	18.3	20.9
Stilfontein	4.95	64.5	100.5	125.7	13.0	20.3	25.4
Southvaal	7.18	55.7	102.5	122.6	7.8	14.3	17.1
Unisel	3.95	–	–	–	–	–	–
Vaalreefs	24.25	273.7	306.6	361.9	11.3	12.6	14.9
Venterspost	2.90	34.2	65.3	80.4	11.8	22.5	27.7
Western Areas	2.17	19.6	32.2	39.7	9.0	14.8	18.3
Western Deeps	11.19	144.2	206.1	236.2	12.9	18.4	21.1
West Driefontein	33.25	439.9	628.3	690.0	13.2	18.9	20.8
Welkom	4.27	63.5	92.5	110.1	14.9	21.7	25.8
Western Holdings	30.00	405.7	522.8	583.1	13.5	17.4	19.4
Winkelhaak	9.75	126.1	175.9	196.0	12.9	18.0	20.1

A Price in US$ as quoted on the London Stock Exchange 1 May 1979

B Dividends paid in US c per share in calendar year 1978 net of 15 percent tax

C Estimate of dividend per share to be paid in 1979 in US ¢ based on a gold value of US $225 per ounce and 1 Rand = US$1.1827

D Estimate of dividend per share to be paid in 1979 in US ¢ based on a gold value of US $240 per ounce and 1 Rand = US$1.1827

E Dividend as a percentage of share price for 1978 ie D as a percentage of A

F C as a percentage of A

G D as a percentage of A

By courtesy of W I Carr, Sons and Co, London

The history of gold

Gold was first mined about 4000 BC but it had been found and used even before that time. Gold is one of the very few metals found in metallic form on the earth's surface as nuggets, and prehistoric man would have found little difficulty in hammering such a nugget into a useful or decorative shape. Although gold has been mined for so many years, over one-third of the amount produced has been mined in the last 30 years.

The earliest uses for gold were restricted to ornamentation and jewllery and it quickly assumed a symbolic significance in early religious ceremonies. The unalloyed metal is too soft to be of much practical use but early written references suggest that gold had already become a symbol of wealth. Although various societies evolved many types of crude currencies such as livestock, shells, iron bars, cloth and salt, the commodities used in sophisticated civilizations as true money were gold and silver.

By the 20th century gold had become the established method of international monetary exchange. Even Karl Marx accepted this use of gold in *Capital* stating: 'A price therefore implies both that a commodity is exchangeable for money, and also that it must be so exchanged. On the other hand, gold serves as an ideal measure of value, only because it has already, in the process of exchange, established itself as the money-commodity. Under the ideal measure of values there lurks the hard cash'.

Lenin however wanted to eliminate gold's monetary role and said that he would use it to line lavatories in Moscow. He was not alone in this view. The economist John Maynard Keynes referred to it as a 'barbarous relic'.

Both silver and gold have been used as money for centuries and much interest has been concerned with the relative values of the two metals. This is often referred to as the bimetallic ratio. Silver, being far less rare than gold, has always been cheaper. About 2700 BC the ratio was nine to one. In 1800 BC in the reign of Hammurabi in Babylon it was six to one. By the sixth century BC it had widened to 12 to one and remained between 12 to one and 16 to one from that time, except in China where there was more gold available than silver and the ratio was about six to one.

Gold was used for international transactions in the time of Hammurabi and was reserved for this purpose, while silver was used for internal reserves and transactions.

Between the 10th Century and the discovery of gold in the New World in the 16th Century, most European gold came from the Alps, Siberia and West Africa (the Gold Coast). Much of Europe's gold was used to buy spices and silk from the Far East.

With the discovery by Cortes of the Aztecs in Mexico and by Pizarro of the Incas in Peru, both immensely rich civilizations in terms of gold, the Spanish and Portuguese missionary zeal became linked to their lust for gold. 'El Dorado', the land of gold, attracted many treasure seekers from the old world who pillaged the gold from the Aztecs and the Incas, hundreds of thousands of whom were massacred in the process. This metal ended the 'gold famine' of the 15th Century. However, the new influx of gold into Europe caused price inflation where the price of commodities became more expensive relative to the price of gold. One major cause of this was the need to send commodities to the people in the new colonies. They required the commodities, which were scarce, but could afford to pay more as they were the source of the gold and silver.

Silver was even more plentiful than gold in America, notably from the mines at Potosi (Bolivia and Peru). The silver/gold ratio in the second half of the 16th Century became 14 to one.

Gold and silver were fuelling the European economies. American silver was cheap and plentiful. It was shipped out to the east where it was highly valued and paid for in goods required by Europe. India was acquiring gold and silver by selling cotton cloth and Japan, which had been an insignificant producer and exporter of these precious metals became more active in both these areas. China which had tried to replace silver and gold with paper money found that the rapid inflation of the 15th Century brought them back to a system based on silver and gold.

Before the gold rush in California in 1849 most gold was still being produced in the Old World, notably by Russia. The Californian discoveries were followed swiftly by the gold rush in Australia where the biggest gold nugget that has ever been found was mined in 1858 at Ballarat. It weighed 83 kilograms and in those days was worth only £8,376.

The South African gold rush began in 1886. Miners had looked for gold before that time but were sidetracked by the discovery of diamonds. The South African goldfields differed from those in America and Australia in that the gold is dispersed in tiny particles through a vast field of low grade ore, deep in the ground, and it was the men who had made their fortunes in the diamond mines who had the capital needed to extract it. Even so the poor rate of recovery made it seem that the gold would lie there forever until three Glasgow men patented the MacArthur-Forrest process, enabling up to 96 percent of the metal to be extracted from the ore, using cyanide solution. The boom in deep level mining began and South Africa quickly became the world's largest gold producing country.

On 10th May 1877 a law was passed in England proposed by Lord Liverpool, which paved the way for the Gold Standard and the end to the bimetallic monetary system. Silver currency was limited to sums of up to £50, thus reducing its uses to coin and small transactions.

England was now on the Gold Standard and with the riches from South African production it became even more wealthy. Sir John Clapham in his *History of the Bank of England* described London at this time as 'The creditor of the whole earth'. In 1871 Germany issued a new currency, the Mark, based on gold; Scandinavia demonetized silver in 1874; the Netherlands went on the Gold Standard in 1875; France and Spain in 1876; Russia in 1893; India in 1898 and the United States followed suit with the Gold Standard Act of 1900.

In 1914 China was the only major nation still on the silver standard. Most international balance of payment settlements could be made in the currency of either country or in sterling and gold was only used for settlements during times of international crisis. Strangely, the price of gold in 1914 was the same as it had been in 1717, largely owing to the huge increase in gold production.

The gold standard ended with the onset of World War I. After the war, many countries wanted to return to the gold standard as it represented a return to the peace and prosperity of the 19th Century. In April 1925, Great Britain adopted a gold bullion standard. This was not based, as before, on gold coins in circulation but on the Bank of England buying and selling bullion at fixed prices. However, this system rested on an overvalued pound, and with the worldwide depression and the international discrepancy between balance of payments deficits and internal money supplies, Britain was forced to withdraw from the Gold Standard in September 1931.

In January 1934, President Roosevelt raised the dollar price of gold from US$ 20.67 to $35 an ounce, and the US Treasury announced that it would buy and sell gold to all official institutions for legitimate monetary purposes at this price. The dollar/gold relationship was not firmly established until after the end of World War II with the establishment of the International Monetary Fund (IMF). With the Bretton Woods Agreement of 1944, the members of the IMF (44 countries) established the exchange value of the currencies based on the official gold price in US dollars. This was possible because of the strength of the US economy after the War compared to those of Western Europe and Japan. The stability of the dollar as a reserve asset for foreign countries coupled with increased South African gold production (from just under 15 million ounces in 1940 to approximately 30 million ounces in 1970) allowed the gold/dollar price to remain within a small trading range of $35/ounce for about 28 years. Only in times of turmoil, such as that in China before the communist takeover, did the price break out of this range and reach $70/ounce. However, as the other economies of the world improved, there was resentment and some questioning of the role of the US dollar in the world's monetary system.

In the late 1960s the strength of the gold/dollar relationship deteriorated. The reasons were: the US balance of payments deficit which increased largely as result of the cost of the Vietnam War; the devaluation of the British pound in 1967 which made speculators and money managers feel that the dollar would be reduced in value and that the gold price would increase; it was also felt that if the price of gold did not go up, South African gold production would decrease due to rising costs and investors began to buy gold feeling that it was undervalued at $35/ounce. In March 1968 the London Gold Market was temporarily closed due to hectic interest and the IMF was forced to instigate a new system. The 'two-tier system' evolved which meant that there were two different gold markets. Gold for monetary uses in fixing reserves and for settlements between banks was fixed at $35/ounce but, outside this system, gold was to be allowed to find its own price level, on the free market. The central banks were not allowed to operate in the free market.

This two-tier system operated until the Autumn of 1971 when the IMF met at the Smithsonian Institute in Washington. The result of these meetings was the 'Smithsonian Agreement' in which new exchange rates were agreed against a newly devalued dollar.

All the recent attempts to reduce the role of gold in the world monetary system have only been stop-gap measures. All have included some linkage with gold while denouncing it, in the hope that this would provide more time to find an alternative. Gold continues to be hoarded by people and bought by investors and citizens in troubled areas, and in increasing amounts for jewellery.

The ancient aura of gold remains even today in our advanced technological society.

Gold jewellery

Jewellery which is responsible for approximately 70 percent of gold consumption is not purchased entirely for the quality of workmanship but in many cases for the investment value of the gold itself. In Bangkok or centres in the Middle East such as Jeddah, gold is purchased in the market places by weight. In 1977 more than 300 tonnes or one-fifth of the world market supply entered this area. In India, on the other hand, when prices for gold are high, princes, and the temples sell their gold jewellery and treasures on the market. With the weakness of the US dollar, buying gold in the form of jewellery has been a good investment. However, among holders of hard currency such as the Yen, Swiss Franc, and German Deutsche Mark, demand for gold jewellery has been lower.

As gold is very soft it is usually alloyed with other metals such as nickel, palladium, copper and silver. This is what creates the coloured golds such as red gold (alloyed with copper), green, white and yellow gold (alloyed with silver). Gold is measured for jewellery in carats based on 24 with 24/24 parts being pure. The other standard carat measurements are 22, 18, 14, 10 and 9 with the balance of the metal being hardening alloys. As most jewellery is alloyed gold, countries like Great Britain require a hallmark on all gold jewellery as a protection for the consumer. The four British Assay offices mark the product and this is the consumer's insurance that the article is up to standard.

Other forms of gold jewellery are rolled gold, investment casting and plated gold. Rolled gold is when a sheet of gold is bonded to an alloy base then pressed until it becomes a thin sheet. This is very popular for pens, pencils, and in wire for jewellery. Investment casting is molten gold poured into a plaster mould. Plated gold is made by depositing a thin film of gold electro-chemically on to a metal blank such as brass.

Secondary sources of gold

Gold scrap is an important above ground source of gold. Reclamation of gold is difficult as it normally exists in minute quantities and because it is often alloyed with another metal or plated on to a less desirable material. However, because of its high value and the increased cost of primary mining, it is becoming more worthwhile to recycle. For instance, 10 years ago when computer parts containing gold were redundant, they were thrown out. Today this material is being recycled by specialist refiners but not all material can be, or is, worth the cost of reclaiming.

Recycling of gold scrap is carried out in the countries that are the largest consumers and therefore generators of scrap such as North America, Japan and Europe. To understand the source of this scrap, one must look at the major industrial uses which are in jewellery, electronics, dentistry and coins.

Each source has its own scrap forms:

Jewellery:	sweepings, grindings, filled scrap, flakes, peelings, punchouts, solutions, sludges, wire and wipe rags.
Electronics:	contacts, diodes, foil, paste, plated parts, wire, solutions, powders, printed circuit boards, components, punchouts, resins-plating, transistors, wire and wipe rags.
Dentistry:	alloys, scrap, sweeps and grinds.
Coins:	punchouts, demonetized coin etc.

Many of the new high technological uses of gold are for purposes of space exploration and defence and due to the security nature of these items they may not enter the market for recycling.

Approximately 35-50 percent of a refiners business is tolling agreements. This is when a consumer or merchant returns his generated scrap to the refinery to obtain, at a conversion cost, pure or alloyed metal in return. The balance of scrap is purchased by a refinery to refine and sell on the market. Scrap is usually valued as per sample or on an outturn basis (recovery determined at refinery). There are many factors which determine the value – gold content, other elements such as precious metals, plastics, deleterious elements, and form.

The use of gold in industrial applications is expanding but as it is costly, consumers are developing ways to use less gold while achieving the same results. This will require more sophisticated recovery methods. However, the high prices, increased industrial use, and high cost of primary mining will mean that more recovery from secondary sources is likely to take place.

Gold prices: annual average, 1945-1978 (London fixing)

US dollars/troy ounce

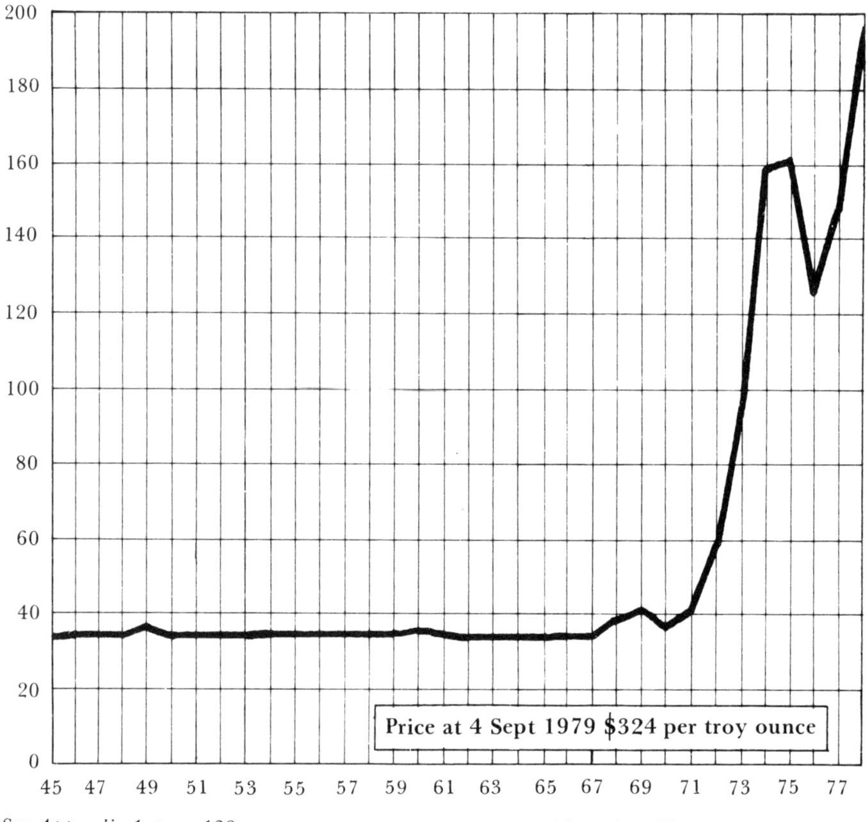

See Appendix 1, page 128

Source: Minerais et Metaux, Consolidated Goldfields and Metal Bulletin

Gold prices: monthly average, 1968-1978 (London fixing)

US dollars/troy ounce

	1968	1969	1970	1971	1972	1973	1974	1975	1976	1977	1978
Jan	35.00	42.30	34.95	37.87	45.75	65.14	129.19	176.27	131.49	132.52	170.50
Feb	35.00	42.61	34.99	38.73	48.26	74.20	150.23	179.59	131.07	136.27	177.80
March	35.00	43.17	35.09	38.87	48.33	84.37	168.42	178.16	132.58	148.29	182.50
April	37.87	43.30	35.02	39.01	49.03	90.50	172.24	169.84	127.94	149.25	175.00
May	40.70	43.47	35.90	40.51	54.62	101.96	163.26	167.39	126.94	146.80	172.50
June	41.13	41.44	35.43	40.10	62.09	120.12	154.10	164.24	125.71	141.10	182.50
July	39.50	41.76	35.33	40.94	65.67	120.17	142.98	165.17	117.76	143.63	185.00
Aug	39.18	41.11	35.38	42.73	67.03	106.76	154.64	162.99	109.93	154.29	205.00
Sep	40.20	40.87	36.19	42.04	65.47	102.97	151.77	144.09	144.15	149.80	207.50
Oct	39.21	40.46	37.54	42.49	64.86	100.08	158.78	142.76	116.14	159.18	222.50
Nov	39.79	37.43	37.45	42.85	62.91	94.92	181.66	142.42	130.46	162.69	220.00
Dec	40.10	35.18	37.46	43.47	63.91	106.72	183.85	139.30	133.88	160.90	212.50
Average	38.56	41.09	35.94	40.80	58.16	97.32	159.26	161.02	124.84	147.98	192.78

Sources: Metal Bulletin and Metals Week

Gold trading: markets

SYDNEY FUTURES EXCHANGE LTD
7th Level, Australia Square Tower
Sydney 2000
Australia
Tel: 02-241 1077 Telex: AA 26713

Chief Executive: W P Nicholas
Gold trading each weekday: 10.30, 14.00 and 15.35
Trading unit: 50 fine troy ozs
Minimum fineness: 0.995 in bars
Prices: in Australian dollars
Delivery: Sydney

THE WINNIPEG COMMODITY EXCHANGE
687-167 Lombard Avenue
Winnipeg, Manitoba
Canada
Tel: 204-9426401 Telex: 07 587778

Chief Executive: D O Ford, President
Gold trading each weekday: 08.15 – 13.30 central time
Trading unit: 100 troy ozs and 400 troy ozs
Minimum fineness: 0.995
Prices: in US dollars
Delivery: Toronto

GOLD EXCHANGE OF SINGAPORE
28th Floor, Clifford Centre
Raffles Place
Singapore 1

Chief Executive: Brian Miller
Gold trading each weekday: 10.00 – 12.30 and 14.30 – 16.30
Trading unit: 100 troy ozs
Minimum fineness: 0.9999
Prices: in US dollars
Delivery: Singapore

CHICAGO BOARD OF TRADE
141 W Jackson Blvd
Chicago
Illinois 60604
Tel: 312-435 3500 Telex: 253223

Chief Executive: Robert K Wilmouth
Gold trading each weekday: 08.25 – 13.35 central time
Trading unit: Three kilos
Minimum fineness: 0.995 in bars
Prices: in US dollars
Delivery: Chicago

CHICAGO MERCANTILE EXCHANGE
444 W Jackson Blvd
Chicago
Illinois 60606
Tel: 312-648 1000
Ext. 326

Chief Executive: Dr Clayton Yeutter
Gold trading each weekday: 08.25 – 13.30
Trading unit: 100 troy ozs
Minimum fineness: 0.995 in bars
Prices: in US dollars
Delivery: Chicago

MID AMERICA COMMODITY EXCHANGE
175 W Jackson Blvd
Chicago
Illinois 60604
Tel: 312-435 0606 Telex: 25296

Chief Executive: David H Morgan, President
Gold trading each weekday: 08.45 – 13.40 central standard time
Trading unit: 33.2 troy ozs (one bar)
Minimum fineness: 0.995
Prices: in US dollars
Delivery: Chicago and New York

COMMODITY EXCHANGE INC (COMEX)
4 World Trade Center
New York
NY 10048
Tel: 212-938 2900 Telex: 12 7066

Chief Executive: Lee H Berendt
Gold trading each weekday: 09.25 – 14.30
Trading unit: 100 troy ozs
Minimum fineness: 0.995
Prices: in US dollars
Delivery: in exchange-licensed vaults

NEW YORK MERCANTILE EXCHANGE
4 World Trade Center
New York
NY 10048
Tel: 212-938 2222

Chief Executive: Richard B Levine
Gold trading each weekday: 09.25 – 14.30 eastern standard time
Trading unit: One kg or 400 troy ozs
Minimum fineness: 0.9995
Prices: in US dollars
Delivery: approved depository in New York

Part 4: Silver

Silver

Silver ore: world production, 1976 *million troy ounces*

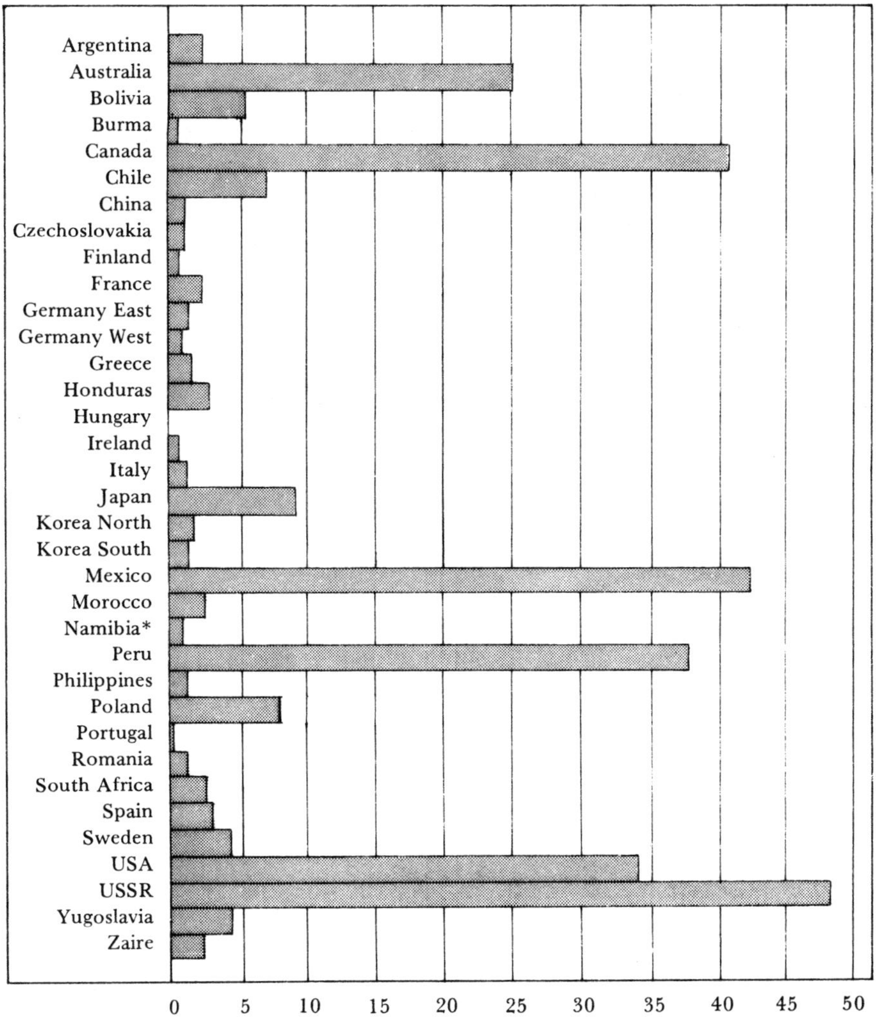

* SW Africa

Source: Metal Bulletin

See Appendix 1, page 129

Grades available

The international weight unit used for silver trading is the troy ounce and silver is traded in bars weighing between 450 and 1,250 troy ounces. The standard minimum purity for the metal traded on the major international commodity markets is 99.9 per cent and the purity of silver is expressed as fineness, pure silver being 1000/1000. Sterling silver has a fineness of 925/1000 and is alloyed with copper, as is silver for coin and plate.

Production method

There are many different silver ores but most of the metal is produced as a by-product of base metal production where silver occurs in sufficient amounts compared with the base metal ore. Silver is most commonly associated with copper, zinc and lead ores but is often found in association with gold. There are also some mines that produce only silver.

Silver in lead/zinc ores is recovered first by allowing the mixture of the molten metals to cool. A crust of the zinc and silver forms on the surface, which is taken off. The zinc is then removed by distillation in a retort. Silver is recovered from copper ores in the electrolytic refining process of the copper: the silver accumulates as a slime at the anode while the copper is being deposited on the cathode. Silver from both these sources is refined by electrolysis, with silver nitrate and nitric acid as electrolyte.

The following table shows the amount of silver produced either in its own right, as primary silver, or as a by-product, in the production of another metal.

Major uses

Silver's use as a medium of monetary exchange has all but died out but some seven per cent of silver supplies are still manufactured into coins each year. This is because the countries in which they are minted traditionally include silver in the alloy used to make them or because they are to be used for commemorative purposes.

Silver's traditional use in jewellery, silver plate, cutlery and objets d'art still represent a major proportion of consumption. In these the silver is almost invariably alloyed with copper to make sterling silver or is plated onto steel. Sterling silver contains 7.5 per cent copper and Sheffield plate is produced by dipping copper plate into molten silver.

The metal is of major industrial value by virtue of its unique physical properties. It is a better conductor than copper of both heat and electricity and is used widely for components in computers, switchgear, thermostats and in many other types of advanced equipment. Some of its salts are light sensitive and form the active ingredient in almost all film emulsions. In photography about half the silver consumed is for making X-ray plates.

Other important uses are in solders; brazing alloys; in the chemical industry as a catalyst; and in pharmaceutical products. Silver also forms a component of one of the new generation of batteries which may represent an important growth area for future consumption.

Silver consumption: world total, 1976

Industrial uses		*million troy ounces*
Canada		6.5
France		19.0
West Germany		42.0
India		18.0
Italy		28.0
Japan		56.0
Mexico		7.0
UK		28.0
US		167.5
Others		23.0
	Total	395.0
Coinage		
Austria		5.5
Canada		6.0
France		5.8
West Germany		1.8
US		1.2
Others		6.6
Total		27.0
Grand Total		422.0

Silver consumption by uses in US, 1977

	million troy ounces	*Percentage*
Electroplated ware	7.2	4.47
Sterling ware	16.6	10.3
Jewellery	8.1	5
Photographic materials	56.0	34.8
Dental/medical supplies	2.0	1.2
Mirrors	2.5	1.6
Brazing alloys/solder	13.7	8.5
Electrical/electronic		
Batteries	6.3	3.9
Contacts/conductors	32.5	20.2
Bearings	0.5	0.03
Catalysts	10.7	–
Coins/medallions and commemorative objects	4.2	2.6
Misc	0.7	.04
Total	161.0	100

Main market features

Between 60 and 70 per cent of the silver consumed in developed countries is used industrially mainly in photography, the electronics industry and as catalysts and solders. Its value is therefore soundly based on its usefulness to industry. The balance is used for tableware and ornamentation (electroplated ware and sterling ware) in jewellery and coinage, etc. Some 27 million ounces of silver are still being used each year to make coinage for currency and for commemorative purposes.

The silver market is unusual in that more silver is consumed annually than is mined, the balance being made up from stocks of silver hoarded by governments and private individuals. This state of affairs cannot last indefinitely but no one really knows exactly how much silver has been hoarded through the centuries in the form of jewellery and plate. India is by far the most important of the countries in which people have traditionally hoarded silver as a form of wealth saving and currency. It has been estimated that the Indians hold 5,000 million ounces of silver, a massive quantity compared with a world annual consumption of around 400 million ounces. The Indian Government banned silver exports in early 1979 at which time silver prices were rising sharply. It is believed that prior to the ban some one million ounces were being exported daily. In the past, however, silver exports from India had not been unduly affected by price rises but more by internal economic forces.

A thriving smuggling trade has been conducted for centuries between India and the Middle East; this has been particularly active whenever the Indian Government has banned exports, but it is unlikely that massive quantities would be unloaded on to the market in the foreseeable future.

The silver market often moves together with that of gold but not always for the same reasons. It is, by tradition, a hedge against currency fluctuations, especially in critical economic conditions, but has not always held its value against major currency falls such as took place between 1974 and 1975. It is also useful for hedging in the very short term. If, for instance, a dealer thinks that sterling is weak against the US dollar he could convert sterling to silver, which has the effect of raising the price of silver in sterling although it stays the same price in terms of dollars. Such transactions constitute a large part of the metal traded in times of fluctuating currency.

Apart from the obvious connection between the gold and silver markets, there is also a connection between silver and soyabeans. Both markets are very important features of the commodities market at the Chicago Board of Trade, and when soyabeans (and grains generally) increase in price it has been traditional for profits to be put into silver. This is not quite as illogical as it sounds as higher food prices increase inflation and silver is as good as any other commodity as a hedge against inflation. Similarly, when soyabean prices drop, dealers may have to sell their silver to make money to pay margin calls, thus lowering the price of silver.

Although there are several important silver markets and other price-fixing institutions around the world, prices rarely get much out of line as there are many silver dealers watching for the opportunity to make profitable arbitrage (selling on one market while simultaneously buying on another) transactions.

Since most silver is recovered as a by-product of the base metal production it is somewhat insensitive to demand. This is because the base metal refiners receive only a small proportion of their income from the sale of silver and are unlikely to produce more copper, lead or zinc simply because the silver price has risen. Silver is, however, widely used in industry, and high silver prices often correspond with high prices of the base metal of which it is a by-product, thus reflecting the general state of the world economic situation.

The investor in silver needs to study several aspects of the market in order to understand price movements. First, the general industrial situation, which is a major influence on prices, since the demand for silver is a fairly accurate barometer of industrial activity. Photography consumes the largest proportion of silver and no economically viable substitute has been found. Second, currency fluctuation – silver prices are more likely to reflect the values of stronger currencies although not necessarily a perfect hedge against inflation. Third, the policies of different governments, that of India particularly, regarding exports or selling from stockpiles. The US Government has now all but exhausted its stockpile of silver. Fourth, the amount of silver being recovered from scrap, including that from demonetizing coins – many governments have been tempted to replace silver-containing coins with less valuable ones or with notes, particularly in times of economic hardship.

Fortunately silver production is widely spread around the world and most of the largest producers are stable countries. Any isolated political or economic crisis in a producing country should not therefore affect the market unduly.

Estimates for the world's silver supply and demand in 1978 and 1979 are about the same. On the supply side, production from mines is expected to rise to 300 million ounces by 1981, but total supplies of silver to the market will be about 380 million ounces. The different will be made up from recovery of scrap of about 80 million ounces; the demonetization of coins accounting for about 15 million ounces; Indian exports (both official and unofficial) for about 30 million ounces; and small sales from other governments making up the rest.

Scrap recovery is bound to become more efficient because of the high value of the metal and the more sophisticated recovery techniques. This will apply especially to recovery of silver from film negatives.

An anomaly, which can only be overcome by the price rising sufficiently to attract more metal into the market, is that at current prices, consumption will continue to be higher by about 25 million ounces per year than the total amount of silver put into the market in 1978/79, some 405 million ounces.

Methods of trading

The marketing of silver, as with gold, was restricted for a long period by price control, linked with its monetary role as coinage. The US Treasury set a 'ceiling' price at which it was prepared to sell silver from its huge surplus stock. This prevented the price from going too high and thus making it worthwhile to melt down coins in circulation. It also effectively controlled market fluctuations by making available an abundance of supplies at a known price.

However, despite successive increases in the price 'ceiling' and the gradual withdrawal of silver for use in coinage throughout most of the world, stocks held by the US Treasury gradually became exhausted. In 1967 the US Treasury finally admitted defeat and after transferring some of its stocks to the strategic stockpile, price control was reluctantly relinquished and the remaining stocks sold to the free market, where values are now left to find their own level.

The disappearance of silver from coinage in most countries of the world has, to a large extent, severed its physical links with the monetary system, but the historical connections remain. Silver is still valued as an alternative store of wealth; a source of protection in times of inflation and currency fluctuations against the depreciation in the value of 'paper' money. It is viewed by many speculators as an alternative investment to gold or platinum, and its price tends to move in the same direction as the gold market. This is not surprising since, historically, silver has been a substitute investment for gold in countries where private citizens were banned from buying gold. This is still the case in Britain.

Speculative investment, use in jewellery, coinage – commemorative medallions and sets – still provide a strong link between silver and gold. But with its removal from the monetary system, silver should logically be viewed as a somewhat unusual industrial metal, unusual in that there is a basic shortfall in new production compared with consumption. This shortfall has to be made up by drawing on stocks built up above the ground over many centuries. It is not as precarious a situation as it might seem. As with many other precious metals silver is fairly indestructible; large quantities are reclaimed from previous uses ranging from coinage to jewellery and photography. So it can be argued that the mining of supplies has merely taken place many years in advance, before the silver is actually needed, and is simply being stockpiled throughout the world by investors against the time when it will be required. The problem is that no one is quite certain where the stocks are, their size and how they can be obtained.

Price is the main mechanism used to procure the surplus supplies stored above the ground in various forms. Market forces find a price level at which holders of stocks are persuaded that it is worthwhile parting with them.There are, however, many diverse influences at work that affect the decision of silver stockholders whether or not to sell, so the pattern of supplies is confused and distorted.

It is further distorted by the fact that mined supplies of silver usually come as a by-product of some other metal not necessarily affected by the price of silver. This means that developments in the silver market do not have the usual effect on mined supplies; the price of silver may rise or fall steeply but makes no impact on the bulk of silver mine production which is influenced by developments in the other metal markets on which decisions to mine or to lower output are based.

The classical free-market mechanism of high prices relieving shortages, and low prices reducing production does not work therefore with mined supplies of silver, but it is very important in controlling the flow of above-the-ground stocks.

Because of the links, albeit now much reduced, with the monetary system physical supplies of silver tend to be channelled through banks and bullion brokers, in addition to the normal supply contracts between mine producers, smelters merchants and consumers. In many cases silver is merely a welcome bonus for mine producers, over and above profits from the main metal, so there is little interest in controlled marketing to specific consumers. The quantities involved are often too small to provoke interest regarding the building up of a producer-consumer relationship, and instead the producer merely disposes of silver at the going market price to any available buyers.

Companies requiring silver for industrial or manufacturing purposes build up regular sources of supply but they have little influence over prices; nor do producers. Prices are basically set in the futures markets in London, Hong Kong, Chicago and New York.

There are two very different markets in London. One is the bullion market, run by the bullion brokers who specialize in the trading of precious metals with monetary connections. Three bullion brokers – Mocatta and Goldsmid, Samuel Montagu and Sharps Pixley – hold a daily 'fixing' each morning when they get together to negotiate the price at which they are prepared to do business bearing in mind orders to buy or sell from their clients.

The fixing prices, quoted for spot delivery and for three, six and twelve months ahead, are only the levels at which business is being transacted daily at a specific time. But they do provide a basis for use in supply contracts between producers and consumers. A producer contracting to deliver certain amounts of silver to a buyer on a regular basis can use, for example, the bullion fixing, on the day of delivery, as a fair current market price.

It is the same mechanism used for fixing the price of gold in London. Indeed the silver bullion brokers are three of the five companies also involved in the London gold fixings. The bullion brokers are responsible for handling the bulk of physical silver traded through London from all parts of the world and in recent years the London bullion dealers have broadened their international trading activities, particularly in respect of the other main trading centres in the United States and Far East. However, in 1968, after the relaxation of the US Treasury control over prices, the London Metal Exchange decided to start trading in silver futures providing an 'open' out-cry market in addition to the secretive fixing.

Initially there was considerable opposition to the idea from the London bullion brokers, who cut their commissions and extended the forward dates in which they were prepared to trade up until 12 months ahead. However, over the years, the two markets have learned to live and co-operate with each other. Trading on the Metal Exchange market, although now confined to three months ahead, is mainly speculative 'paper' futures. It is strongly influenced by trends in the London bullion market and United States futures. Bullion brokers, and silver refiners, nowadays use the Metal Exchange as a 'hedging' medium against price fluctuations and their warehouses provide convenient extra storage capacity for surplus silver stocks. London bullion brokers are now members of the Metal Exchange, and Sharps Pixley was elected a full ring-dealing member at the beginning of 1979.

The Metal Exchange deliberately set the size of the minimum lot that can be traded at a very high level of 10,000 ounces to discourage speculation by individuals, unable to afford large sums of money.

The contract was also launched with a seven months forward delivery quotation – a compromise between those who sought to trade 12 months ahead or more, and the traditionalists who wanted to limit trading to three months forward, as with the Metal Exchange base metals markets. Nor surprisingly the seven months compromise proved a failure and was dropped through lack of interest.

Nevertheless, despite these early difficulties the London Metal Exchange market has established itself as an important influence in world silver trading. It provides open and unrestricted trading facilities both for a hedging against unpredictable price fluctuations and for speculators wishing to invest in silver.

It is particularly useful for European silver traders, being open during normal office hours, unlike the markets in the United States, or the Far East.

In addition, London is very useful to silver traders and investors in the United States as a safety valve, if the markets in Chicago and New York move either the permissible limit up or down when trading is officially suspended. Instead of being trapped in a market from which it may be difficult to get out without incurring heavy losses, traders can switch to either the London bullion market or the Metal Exchange, where there is no restriction on price movements.

A great deal of arbitrage business – that is trading the same commodity in two markets when their prices diverge – is also carried out between London and the US markets.

However, it is fair to say that normally world silver prices are controlled by trends in the US futures markets. The two main markets – on the New York Commodities Exchange (Comex) and on the Chicago Board of Trade – attract such a huge volume of business that it swamps normal trading activity on markets in the rest of the world. The London bullion brokers, Metal Exchange dealers, European traders including the Swiss Banks, do play a very important role in silver trading and on occasions push the price in a certain direction. But the trend is set usually by the huge flow of funds in the United States, especially from private investors eager to make a profit by anticipating market movements correctly, or alternatively seeking protection for their funds by investing in silver.

Because of the United States dominance of price trends, silver is viewed very much as a 'dollar' commodity and therefore reacts very quickly to changes in the value of the dollar. But there are a host of other influences connected with silver's role as an important industrial metal. These include supply/demand considerations such as the rate of silver exports from India and the general outlook for the main silver-using industries, notably photography and electronics.

In recent years the importance of the Far Eastern silver markets, especially in Hong Kong, has been increasing strongly.

A feature of the silver futures markets is that the abundance of supplies above the ground, available for immediate delivery, virtually always keeps the cash (or spot) price at a discount to the quotations for delivery at a future date. The gap between the cash price and forward quotations is regulated by current interest rates. Traders are constantly alert for the times when the cash price discount becomes too wide, allowing a guaranteed profit to be made by simultaneously buying cash silver at a low price and selling it back to the market some time ahead – three, six or 12 months – at a higher price.

The guaranteed profit is the difference between the cash and forward price, after allowing for deductions to cover the cost of storage, insurance and brokers' commissions until the cash silver is sold back to the market. This is known as a cash-and-carry transaction. When the prices are right it is a method of obtaining a profit which exceeds the rate of interest, that would have been earned during the period concerned, by normal inter-bank transactions. Cash-and-carry transactions are used mainly by large financial institutions, including banks, which can gain considerably by obtaining even a slight advantage in interest rates. It can also be used by private investors.

There have been times – notably when the Bunker Hunt family in the United States was alleged to be trying to corner the market by buying up available supplies – when the cash price has been equal to or even exceeded forward quotations. But this is very unusual and unlikely to last for long in view of the surplus stocks above the ground already mined.

Silver's transition from being a monetary symbol to an industrial metal together with the greater freedom to buy gold in recent years, has tended to tarnish the attraction of silver for investment purposes. It is being viewed increasingly as just another commodity, if slightly unusual because of the permanent production deficit.

Unlike gold in times of inflation, currency instability and economic recession, silver tends to be in lesser rather than greater demand at these times because of its dependence on sales to industry.

However, this is also a strength. In times of high industrial activity silver is in greater demand while its monetary connections stop it from becoming too depressed during periods of recession. At the same time and working in its favour as long-term investment is the fact that consumption continues to outstrip new production each year, despite the great improvement in reclaiming previously used 'scrap' silver.

The lower unit price of silver, compared with gold and platinum, means that it is available to a much wider investment public, either for physical purchases or through paper transactions on the futures markets, including options.

Silver Coins

By 1965 most countries had demonetized silver coinage. This was done immediately after a huge increase in coin production, especially in the United States, to feed the growing demand for their use in slot machines. Some idea of the subsequent dramatic drop in silver consumption can be gauged from the following figures: in the years 1963/64 and 1965 more than 800 million ounces were used; in 1975/76 and 1977 the figure was only 80 million ounces.

In recent years the greatest use for silver in coinage has been for commemorative purposes. Examples of this are the German Olympic Medal 1971/72, which is a 5 DM piece, 625/1000 silver, balance copper; the Canadian Olympic coins for the 1976 Olympic Games; and the

United States bicentennial coins minted in 1975/76. The Soviet Union also intends to produce a silver coin to commemorate the 1980 Olympic Games but consumption for this purpose can be met by USSR silver production. Mexico produces a 100 peso silver coin, which consumes about five million ounces per year.

Unlike gold, the citizens of most countries are not prevented from buying silver in any form including bullion (ingots). This has averted the development of any large-scale market in silver coins.

The history of silver

Although most silver is found naturally in the form of complex compounds, often in association with less rare metals such as copper, lead and zinc, it is occasionally found as nuggets in the pure metallic state. This is known as native silver and it was almost certainly this form of silver that was first discovered and used by man some 4000 years BC, slightly later than the discovery of gold and copper.

The first uses of silver were decorative, but inscriptions in the Royal Tombs of Chaldaea made in the fourth millenium BC imply that silver had already become a means of monetary exchange.

The earliest known mines were in Asia Minor where the metal was found as native silver or as silver chloride which could be easily converted to bullion in a charcoal fire. Silver was being mined in Greece and the Aegean Islands by 1000 BC and silver ornaments and jewellery, dating from as far back as 2500 BC, have been found all over the Mediterranean area.

Silver played an important role in trade in the ancient world. references to Abraham using silver pieces are made in the Bible and the Babylonian 'talent' certainly contained silver. But it was the Greeks who popularized the use of silver as a medium of exchange, in the form of minted coinage.

The Romans mined silver throughout their Empire and made it the basis of their monetary system. Much of their silver was mined in Spain but later a shortage of the metal encouraged them to debase their coins with copper and other metals until there was almost no silver left in them by the end of the Roman era.

Until the discovery, by the Spanish and Portuguese explorers, of vast deposits of silver in America in the sixteenth century, Europe remained very short of the metal. This encouraged the alchemists to try to find some way of synthesizing it from other materials. They referred to the metal as lunia and gave it the symbol of a crescent moon, which is used today by the London Metal Exchange to denote the metal.

The most famous early silver mines in America were Potosi in Bolivia, and Guanajuato and Pachuca in Mexico. Bolivia's output exceeds one billion ounces and was the world's largest silver producing country until

1700.

The discovery of large silver deposits in America helped to cause high inflation in Europe in the 17th and early 18th centuries because the silver was needed to buy spices and cloth from the East, and had to be bought from America with expensive manufactured goods.

Interest in silver as a measure of wealth has lasted in the East to this day. Indians for instance have hoarded more of the metal than the rest of the world put together. In the 18th century a large trade began between American countries, particularly Mexico, and the Far East, with the exchange of silver for silk, cotton and porcelain.

Large silver deposits were discovered in Nevada in 1859 making the United States the world's largest producer between 1871 and 1900. Mexico was the largest producer from 1900 to 1968, since when Canada has rivalled Mexico for this distinction.

In 1873 when the United States was producing more silver than any other country, together with huge quantities of gold, the Government found itself in a dilemma. It could either join Great Britain and the rest of the world in the Gold Standard, which might have weakened the links between the Eastern States and the Western States which produced silver, or it could decide against going on the Gold Standard which might reduce the might of the United States as a trading nation. The dilemma was resolved by opting to put the dollar on the Gold Standard, and various legislative measures were approved at the same time to support the silver price with government purchases. This legislation was repealed by President Kennedy's administration in 1961. It was only in 1965 that the Johnson Silver Coinage Act finally demonetized silver completely and, with the exception of Bicentennial coins, all newly minted coins in the United States were made of cupronickel. In 1976 the US Government decided to sell its remaining silver stockpile of 139.5 million ounces which will take some years to complete, especially as full congressional authorization for this sale has not yet been granted.

Many large silver producing countries would like silver to retain an important role in coinage production and monetary transactions but present trends suggest that the uses for silver in industry, and for jewellery and tableware will more than adequately account for estimated future production.

Silver jewellery and plate

Approximately five percent of all silver used each year is for jewellery with electroplated ware, sterling ware, and commemorative objects responsible for another 17 percent. Silver jewellery and plate enjoy a good market, though not as good as the gold market. Silver does have a tendency to tarnish as it reacts with oxygen.

Silver jewellery is in the form of plate or cast. Plated silver is 99.9 percent pure and is plated onto a blank such as steel or nickel silver. Nickel silver is actually a nickel copper alloy and contains no silver. Silver plating is carried out by placing an anode consisting of 99.9 percent silver into a chemical bath containing silver potassium cyanide and other chemicals like brighteners and hardeners. A cathode which is the object to be plated is placed in the bath. When current is passed through the cathode, silver moves from the anode and is deposited on the cathode. The amount of coating depends on the length of time in the bath. The coating is measured in microns sometimes as little as seven or as much as 20-25. The British and the French are often considered the best platers as they plate in the range of 20-25 microns. This means that the object does not wear out as quickly.

Cast silver is normally sterling silver which contains 92.5 percent silver and 7.5 percent copper and therefore contains more silver by weight than a plated item. Sterling silver objects in the United Kingdom must be hallmarked in order to maintain the standard and protect the consumer. Quality can vary considerable throughout the world, so it is best to be careful when purchasing silver objects. Sterling silver is considered the better investment – whereas silver plate has doubled in price in the last 20 years, sterling silver's value is twenty times that.

Secondary sources of silver

Some 70 to 80 million ounces of silver per year are generated from secondary sources and this represents approximately 18-20 percent of annual supplies to the market. The most active areas are the United States, Japan and Western Europe because of their high industrial use of silver. India at times also provides silver by the melting down of jewellery when silver prices are high. In the last few years there has been a shortfall between production and consumption with consumption gradually increasing and a relatively fixed production of scrap which therefore has become an important source.

For the sources of the silver scrap, its industrial uses need to be examined. The biggest industrial use of silver is in the photographic industry where a large proportion can be recovered from scrap film and spent developing solutions. This is available from large developing firms and hospitals, in the form of X-rays and developing solutions. In the 1960s there was a major effort in recovery from these sources and processes have been developed with a high recovery rate.

Another obvious area is the jewellery trade where scrap is generated in plating solutions, sweeps, grindings, wire, old jewellery and plate, and punchouts. After refining this is most often returned in the form of a workable product to the customer who generated the scrap. The electrical industry generates scrap in the process of producing electrical

Silver prices: annual average, 1945-1978
US dollars/troy ounce

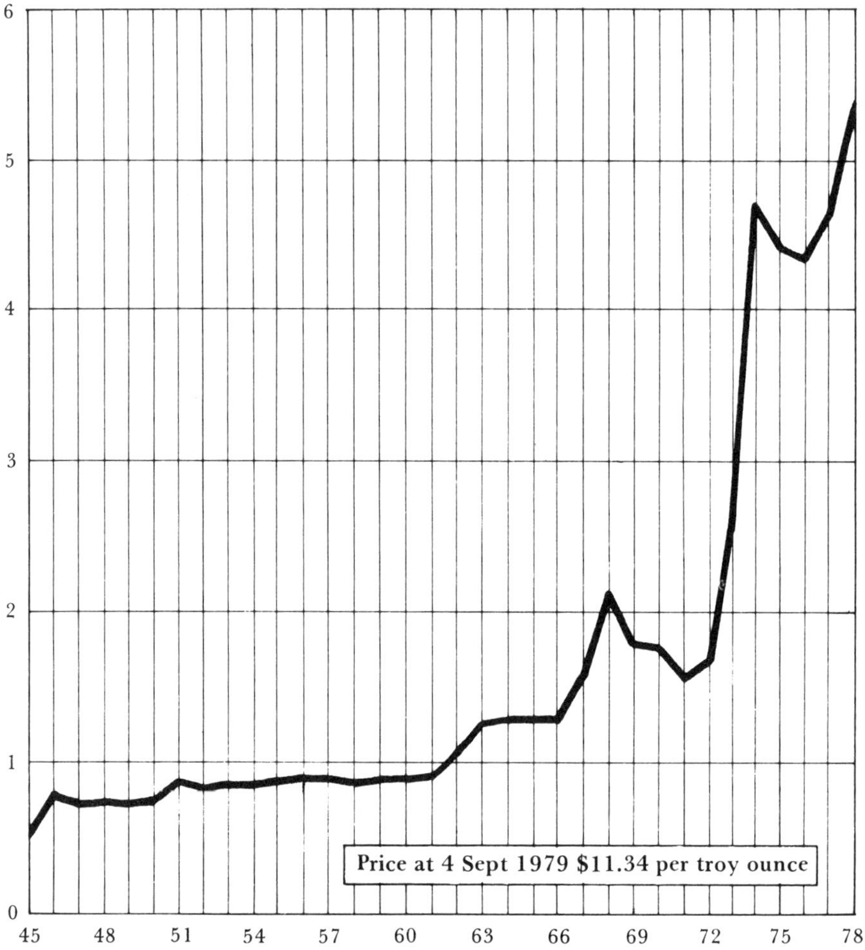

See Appendix 1, page 131

Sources: J Aron – American Bureau of Metal Statistics, Metal Bulletin, Metals Week and Handy and Harman.

switches and batteries and these products are themselves frequently scrapped. In electronics the silver is usually alloyed with something like copper, cadmium or platinum group metals. In batteries it is mostly a zinc, cadmium or copper alloy. These other alloying elements must be taken into consideration in the process of refining scrap.

Other important sources are in dentistry, in the form of dental alloys, dental scrap and wire; also in the form of bearings scrap, spent silver catalysts, and brazing (solder) alloys; and in the demonetization of silver coins which provide three to four percent of annual supplies. This last area of recovery was particularly significant in the United States in 1974 and again in 1976 when approximately 55 million ounces was generated, largely due to demonetization in Germany and the high price of silver.

In considering the secondary sources of silver it is important to note the following factors:

- The price of silver: when it is high more silver is recovered and when it is low the position is reversed.
- The level of industrial activity
- Alloying agents or deleterious elements combined with silver
- The return of refined silver scrap directly to the consumer
- The fact that as the price increases consumers attempt to use less silver in their products.

Silver trading: markets

THE LONDON METAL EXCHANGE
Whittington Avenue
London EC3V 1LB
Tel: 01 626 3311 Telex: 895 1367
Cables: METMA LONDON EC3

Chairman of the Board: Mr P.G. Smith, CBE
Silver trading each weekday:
12.05 – 12.10
13.00 – 13.05
15.40 – 15.45
16.25 – 16.30
Trading unit: 10,000 oz
Minimum fineness: 0.999 in bars 450-1250 troy ozs
Minimum price movement: £0.001 (0.1 of a penny per troy oz)
Delivery: Amsterdam, Hamburg, London and Rotterdam
Dealing by ring dealing members (brokers)

CHICAGO BOARD OF TRADE
141 W Jackson Blvd
Chicago
Illinois 60604
Tel: 312 435 3500 Telex: 253223

Chief Executive: Robert K Wilmouth
Silver trading each weekday:
08.40 – 13.25 US central time
Trading unit: 5000 troy ozs
Price: in US dollars and cents, minimum fluctuation 0.1 cents per troy oz
Minimum fineness: 0.999 in bars of 1000 ounces + or - 109
Delivery: Chicago

MID AMERICA COMMODITY EXCHANGE
175 Jackson Blvd
Chicago
Illinois 60604
Tel: 312 435 0606 Telex: 25296

Chief Executive: David H Morgan – President
Silver trading each weekday:
08.45 – 13.40 US central time
Trading unit: 1000 troy ozs
Minimum fineness: 0.995 in 1000 troy oz bars
Delivery: Chicago

COMMODITY EXCHANGE INC (COMEX)
4 World Trade Center
New York
NY 10048
Tel: 212 938 2900 Telex: 12 7066

Chief Executive: Lee H Berendt
Silver trading each weekday:
10.00 – 14.15 eastern standard time
Trading unit: 5000 troy ozs
Minimum fineness: 0.999 in bars of 1000 ozs
Delivery: in any exchange-licenced warehouse

Silver prices: monthly average, 1967-1978 (New York)

US cents/troy ounces 999 purity

	1967	1968	1969	1970	1971	1972	1973	1974	1975	1976	1977	1978
Jan	129.30	198.99	197.89	187.65	163.96	146.96	201.66	363.70	419.25	406.27	437.50	490.00
Feb	129.30	185.47	183.97	189.58	160.03	150.36	223.62	535.90	435.69	408.64	455.50	492.50
March	129.30	218.05	182.57	188.85	166.90	153.08	230.92	532.55	433.15	418.91	475.00	525.00
April	129.30	220.38	177.81	185.29	172.60	157.20	220.72	503.60	420.92	435.55	465.00	525.00
May	129.59	237.68	176.10	167.00	166.67	158.31	240.12	543.18	453.81	448.85	467.50	507.50
June	130.10	246.41	164.55	163.94	160.81	156.90	262.09	489.61	448.91	481.17	435.00	532.50
July	159.29	231.38	161.83	168.66	158.08	173.58	270.56	441.55	470.46	477.36	450.00	525.00
Aug	174.98	219.46	165.26	179.77	158.66	184.61	263.65	443.14	492.51	423.71	447.40	550.00
Sept	167.95	220.85	178.55	180.16	142.14	177.67	267.51	404.88	451.60	429.52	460.00	547.50
Oct	178.59	197.28	187.25	174.58	133.58	181.06	283.56	482.98	432.89	422.51	482.50	585.00
Nov	195.32	201.78	192.31	176.04	131.99	183.25	285.99	469.39	433.24	436.91	487.50	590.00
Dec	206.00	195.93	180.71	163.48	139.35	197.60	313.67	439.13	408.49	434.76	467.50	597.50
Average	154.97	214.46	179.07	177.08	154.56	168.38	255.34	470.80	441.85	435.35	460.87	538.95

Source: J. Aron, American Bureau of Metal Statistics

Part 5: Platinum group metals

Platinum

Platinum: world production, 1976 *troy ounces x 10,000*

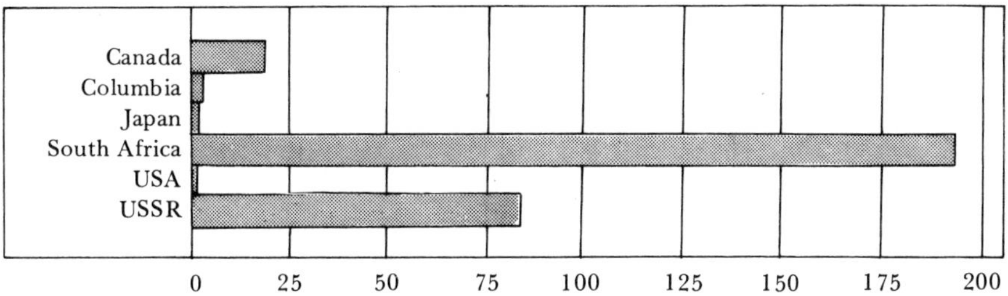

Reserves 209 million ounces *See Appendix 1, page 132*

Grades available

The generally accepted minimum purity of platinum traded on the dealer market is 99.9 percent, although most producers offer material of about 99.95 percent minimum. The minimum standard of 99.89 percent, previously accepted, is rapidly being considered as low-grade material.

The most commonly traded forms of platinum are plates of about 50 troy ounces and ingots of about five kilos. Other commonly traded forms are sponge (irregular granules), sheet, wire and powder. These forms are traded at discounts or premiums to the plate and ingot market depending on the extra, or reduced, costs to the producer and the requirement of the buyer.

Production method

Platinum does not naturally combine with any other element but is almost invariably found in association with nickel and copper ores or with gold. Their platinum content is minute, and several tonnes may have to be treated to recover a single ounce. This is the main reason for platinum's exceptionally high value. These platinum-containing minerals usually have equally small concentrations of gold and other platinum group metals.

Platinum-rich concentrates are recovered during the electrolytic refining process of the metal with which it is associated in the ores. These concentrates are dissolved in aqua regia and the platinum precipitated with ammonium chloride after first precipitating the gold with ferrous sulphate. The resulting platinum chloride is then reduced to form sponge which can be melted to form ingots.

Major uses

Apart from its use in jewellery, platinum has a large range of very important industrial uses, in spite of its very high price.

It has many applications as a catalyst, either in its pure form or as an alloy with rhodium or absorbed in other materials such as asbestos. Platinum catalysts are used in achieving a large range of chemical reactions such as that of reforming petroleum; producing nitric acid; producing some pharmaceutical products; and for removing hydrogen and chlorine, particularly in organic chemical synthesis.

Pieces of platinum puntured with extremely small holes are used as spinarets for extruding man-made fibres such as nylon, rayon and glass fibres. Platinum and platinum alloyed with other platinum group metals are used to make thermocouples, used to measure temperature, and in thermostats. It is also used in many other electronic components and devices.

Platinum's incorruptibility makes it the perfect material for crucibles and retorts which are used in handling highly corrosive chemicals or where reistance to high temperatures is required. It is also used to make a range of structural alloys for specialist components used in machines which run at high temperatures.

Main market features

The most significant factor concerning platinum production is that about 85 per cent of Western supplies are produced in South Africa, which therefore has a considerable control over the market. It can limit production to meet demand or, alternatively, increase prices in times of high demand. This does not mean that South Africa is able to increase or diminish production instantaneously; new mining and refinery capacity is extremely expensive and takes several years to complete. Furthermore, South Africa relies heavily on income from the export of minerals, not least of which is platinum, but it does mean that, within certain limits, the prices cannot fall too drastically except for short periods of time when investors outside South Africa lose confidence in their platinum holdings.

Platinum consumption, 1977

	troy ounces 1000
US non-automotive	425
Automotive	375
Total US	800
Japan net imports	1090
reduction in stocks	40
Total Japan	1130
Other countries (Est)	750
Total non-communist world	2680

Platinum supplies against consumption, 1977

Supply	
South African production	1750
Canadian production	120
USSR sales to the West	575
Miscellaneous, including recycled scrap, release from inventories, etc (est)	220
Total supply	2665
Apparent surplus (+) or short full (–)	–15

Source: Financial Mail

Platinum consumption by uses in US, 1976

	troy ounces
Automotive	480,000
Chemical	100,000
Petroleum	65,000
Glass	42,000
Electrical	82,000
Dental/Medical	35,000
Jewellery/Decorative	25,000
Misc. and undistributed	74,000
Total	903,000

Source: American Bureau of Metal Statistics, Inc.

As an investment, platinum is more solidly based than gold: it is a more useful metal and its physical properties are such that it is far more difficult to find substitutes for its uses in industry.

Consumption patterns, however, vary considerably from country to country. In Japan, for instance, platinum is considered to be more fashionable than gold for jewellery and about 70 percent of platinum consumption is used for that purpose; but in the United States less than 10 percent is used in jewellery production. Both countries have about the same level of platinum consumption and are by far the largest consumers.

In most other industrialized countries the consumption pattern is similar to that in the United States: over 80 percent of all platinum produced is consumed industrially. This compares very favourably with gold of which the industrial consumption is approximately 17 percent.

There is some difficulty in obtaining accurate figures covering platinum group metal production in the USSR. Since the beginning of 1977 the Soviet Union has been reducing sales of platinum to the West and a number of reasons are put forward to explain this. First, that between 125,000 and 250,000 ounces will be used to produce 1980 Olympic commemorative coins; second, that the Soviet Union and other Eastern European countries have a greater internal demand (probably in the petrochemical industry where platinum is used as a catalyst); third, that the Soviet Union is stockpiling platinum (perhaps on the theory that a disruption in South Africa will limit supplies); fourth, that much Russian platinum is a by-product of nickel production, and since the demand for nickel has been at a very low ebb for several years nickel, and consequently platinum, production has been reduced; and fifth, that a number of mines have collapsed or have been depleted.

Whatever the reasons, new Russian sales of platinum have almost ceased: only long-term supply contracts made in the past are being honoured. In 1976 Russian sales to the West were estimated to be between 450,000 and 630,000 ounces, an extremely large quantity to be withdrawn from the market.

Most dealers suggest that Russian sales of platinum might be withheld indefinitely and that they will be resumed only in the form of semi-fabriacted items such as gauze used in catalytic chemical reactions and in the form of commemorative coins. It is expected that the quantities sold in these forms will be much smaller.

Another factor affecting supply that must be taken into consideration is South Africa's political instability. Even if the possibility of a complete collapse of the South Africa economy were ruled out, it has been suggested, both within and outside that country, that the South African Government might use platinum supplies as a lever to obtain essential supplies, such as oil, or deny platinum supplies to countries who might impose sanctions against South Africa.

If this occurs at a time when the Western world expects South African production to increase in order to cover the withdrawal of Russian supplies, the market would be seriously depleted.

Nickel prices rose sharply in 1979 from the very low levels reached in 1978, and since platinum is produced as a by-product of nickel production in the Soviet Union, Canada and South Africa, platinum production could increase slightly.

In view of the growing strategic importance of platinum, combined with the political unreliability of its sources, several Western governments have begun to consider the possibility of stockpiling the metal. So far the United States, Germany, France and Sweden have acted on this proposition. Historically, stockpiling has been carried out in a manner to avoid any disrupting effect on the market but it would be difficult for any country to buy sufficient quantities to form an effective stockpile without dramatically increasing the price in the present market. Nevertheless such action must be considered.

Although several other Western countries do produce small quantities of platinum there is no source that could replace South Africa if any long-term disruption should occur.

Automobile catalytic converters

In the mid-1970s the US Government passed legislation to control the level of toxic fumes emitted by motor cars. All motor cars produced in the United States and any that were imported after 1975, are required, by law, to have modified exhaust systems to reduce fumes to certain low levels. This is done by incorporating a catalytic converter consisting of ceramic beads coated with platinum which consumes approximately 350,000 ounces of platinum per year in the United States. About 100,000 ounces per year is used for the same purpose in Japan, particularly for cars exported to the United States.

Incorporated in this legislation is a provision to reduce car pollution even further in 1980. This may require a different type of catalyst using other platinum group metals, especially as the inclusion of converters in exhaust systems produces an added benefit in fuel saving. There is, however, some contention in US Government circles regarding the overall benefits of this legislation since the dramatic rise in platinum prices.

Catalytic converters can be used only with petrol which contains no lead (unleaded gas). It sells for a few cents more per gallon than lead-containing petrol and is not readily available at all petrol stations. In recent times, in consequence of the petrol shortage, US motorists have been ripping out their converters in order to be able to use the more easily obtainable leaded petrol.

Platinum in the petroleum industry

When certain lead compounds are added to fuel they have the effect of increasing the octane rating. This saves the effort and cost of normal catalytic reforming processes in which platinum catalysts are used.

The growing concern about lead pollution in the atmosphere may reverse the present trend and lead to the use of more expensive high octane fuels, which would require more platinum. At the moment the United States uses about 100,000 ounces per year for this purpose.

Efforts are being made to find substitutes for the 'anti-pinking' lead compounds used as fuel additives, and innovations in engine design may reduce the necessity for high octane fuels.

Platinum coins

The only important platinum coins are those minted in the USSR which are of 99.9 percent purity. The current edition, produced to commemorate the 1980 Olympic Games, have a face value of 150 roubles.

The history of platinum

Platinum was known in its impure state from early times; however, it was not used because of its high melting point and the difficulty in working the metal with the methods known at the time. It has been discovered in many areas of the world – Brazil, Columbia, Peru, the Soviet Union, Australia, Borneo, Tasmania, the United States, Canada and South Africa though the largest producers are the Soviet Union, Canada and South Africa.

The history of platinum really began with its major discovery in South Africa in 1923 by a farmer in the Waterbery District, though it had already been discovered in Russia in the early 19th century. This began a period of exploitation which can only be described as a 'platinum rush' which is an important part of the history of South Africa itself. The initial deposit was called the Merensky Reef, named after the geologist who developed the area. After this came the discovery of other important areas such as Lydenburg, Potgietersrust and Rustenburg. Towns were built to support these mining areas and prominent names such as those of Ernest Oppenheimer, Anglo American, Johannesburg Consolidated Investments, Rustenburg Platinum Union, and Consolidated Goldfields were involved with the exploitation. They all sought platinum deposits, exploited mines, and bought into each other. Today the three major producers are Rustenburg Platinum (estimate production one million ounces per annum), Impala Platinum (estimated annual production 800,000 ounces), and Western Platinum (estimated annual production 75,000 ounces). Canada is now the second largest producer in the Western world. The USSR, which has an estimated annual production of 700,000 ounces, is the second largest producer overall.

Platinum jewellery

Platinum jewellery is responsible for 20-30 percent of the world's consumption of platinum. It is not as popular as gold or silver though its strength was responsible for its use in rings to hold stones. It can be substituted with rhodium-plated white gold. Platinum is particularly popular for jewellery in Japan.

Platinum jewellery is usually alloyed to make it harder. To be hallmarked in the United Kingdom the purity must be 95 percent. Since platinum is a more dense metal, platinum jewellery contains more precious metal by size than does gold jewellery for instance.

Jewellery represents the best growth area for platinum consumption.

Secondary sources of platinum

Platinum scrap has an important role in platinum supplies not because of the supply/demand relationship, since supply is fairly balanced with demand, but because of its high price and the ability to recycle material back to the generating industries in the form of prime product. The major generating industries for platinum scrap are those using catalysts (the automotive, chemical and petroleum industries); jewellery and electrical industries together with such minor areas as the glass and dental industries. It is important to remember that the platinoids are produced with platinum and that these are a main alloying agent with platinum in its various uses.

In 1975, in the United States, automobiles were mass produced for the first time with catalytic converters attached. These converters were developed to reduce emissions of carbon monoxide and hydrocarbons. The element necessary to achieve this result is basically platinum together with some palladium, which has since been altered to a platinum/palladium/rhodium alloy. This use of platinum now accounts for almost 25 percent of the platinum consumption annually, though only approximately 1.3 to 2 grams of platinum group metals (pgm) is used per car. In 1979/80 it is expected to increase to 2. to 2.4 grams of pgm per car. However, considering that some 25 million cars were produced with these catalytic converters, about 1.1 million of pgm has been used, with the bulk of it being platinum.

How much pgm will be left after use is not known but a conservative estimate is 50 percent, or a half a million pgm of converter scrap, which will not be available until the 1975 production automobiles begin to be scrapped. It is felt by the main platinum catalyst producer (Matthey Bishop, the marketing arm for Rustenburg in the United States which is Johnson Matthey in the United Kingdom) that this could provide an estimated 200,000 ounces per annum by 1983 and a half million ounces by 1992. This is obviously a substantial quantity. There is some doubt, however, whether the companies involved in scrap cars will make the effort, or are sophisticated enough, to reclaim this material. Another factor is that, with only approximately 2 grams of pgm per converter, the price of the platinum, palladium and rhodium will have to remain very high to make recycling worthwhile.

Platinum catalysts have an important function in the chemical industry and as part of the refining process in the petroleum industry. Individual consumers have their own proprietary platinum and pgm alloy, details of which are usually known only to themselves and the producer. When these catalysts become 'spent' (used up), they are normally returned to the prime producer who refines the spent catalysts and returns the prime product to the consumer. This material is an important secondary source but is not a factor in the free market. It is a source that is difficult to quantify as it is a closely protected producer-consumer transaction.

As jewellery is responsible for 30-40 percent of the platinum market it is also a secondary source in the form of jewellery sweeps, grindings, casting scrap, plating solutions, redundant jewellery and decorative objects. A great deal of it is recycled to the prime producer in return for product.

The electrical industry in production and in redundant products

Platinum prices: annual average, 1945-1978 (New York) free market

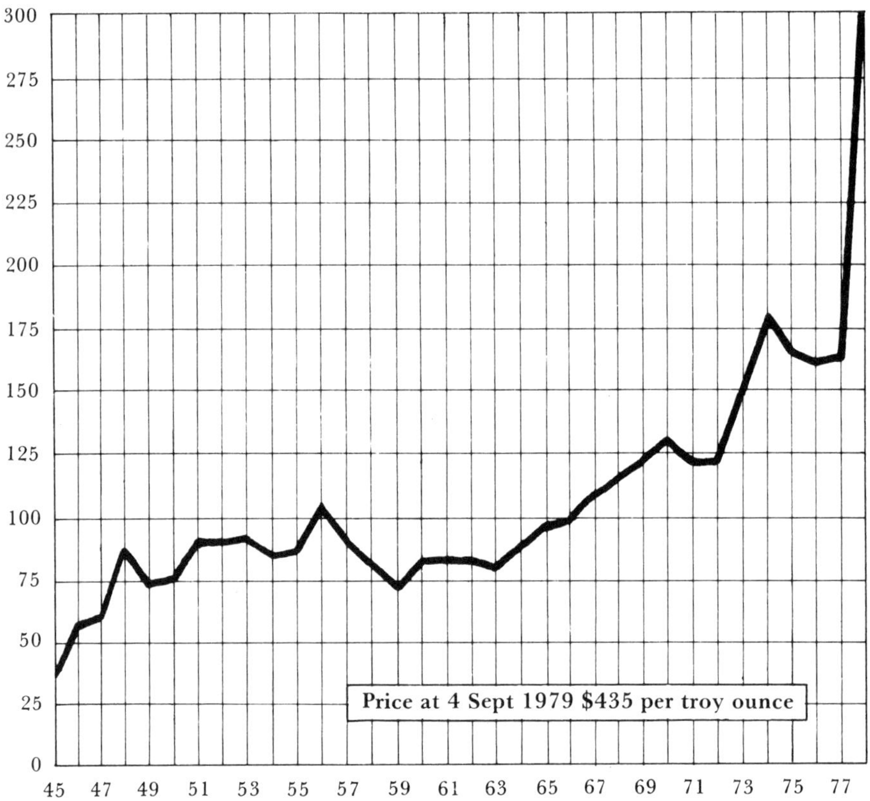

See Appendix 1, page 132

Sources: Metal Bulletin, Metals Week, Minerais et Metaux

Platinum prices: monthly average, 1969-1978 (New York/London)

US dollars/troy ounce

	1969	1970	1971	1972	1973	1974	1975	1976	1977	1978
Jan	122.50	132.50	129.00	122.50	132.50	162.68	195.00	160.00	154.65	201.80
Feb	122.50	132.50	122.50	122.50	141.97	172.50	180.53	160.00	161.26	223.79
March	122.50	132.50	122.50	122.50	152.50	172.50	175.00	160.00	163.09	226.69
April	122.50	132.50	122.50	122.50	152.50	172.50	163.06	160.00	160.80	213.86
May	122.50	132.50	122.50	122.50	152.50	174.55	160.00	160.00	156.40	233.16
June	122.50	132.50	122.50	122.50	152.50	195.00	160.00	163.64	149.96	244.93
July	122.50	132.50	122.50	128.00	152.50	195.00	162.73	175.60	149.12	247.04
Aug	122.50	132.50	122.50	132.50	152.50	195.00	175.00	182.50	146.84	267.36
Sept	122.50	132.50	122.50	132.50	152.50	195.00	175.00	182.50	150.46	270.02
Oct	122.75	132.50	122.50	132.50	160.50	195.00	172.17	182.50	157.94	332.27
Nov	132.50	132.50	122.50	132.50	160.50	195.00	160.00	167.00	167.60	328.78
Dec	132.50	132.50	122.50	132.50	160.50	195.00	160.00	167.00	176.72	340.28
Average	124.18	132.50	123.04	127.13	139.25	184.98	169.87	168.40	157.91	260.83

Sources: Metal Bulletin, Metals Week, American Metal Market

is another source of scrap. The high value of platinum makes it profitable to reclaim it from clad materials, contacts, pastes, powders, magneto points, spark plugs and thermoplastic wire.

Other sources of platinum scrap are dental alloys, dental scrap in the form of sweeps and grindings and laboratory ware. However, as with all precious metal scrap the value is determined by samples or recovery and the subsidiary alloyed metals and other non-metallic elements must be taken into consideration. This is particularly true of platinum, which is often alloyed with another pgm or non-metallic substance. Examples of this are the catalysts that rely on clay, ceramic and zeolite supports.

Platinum trading: market

NEW YORK MERCANTILE EXCHANGE
4 World Trade Center
New York
NY 10048
Tel. 212 938 2222

Chief Executive: Richard B. Levine
Platinum trading each weekday:
9-30 – 14.10 eastern standard time
Trading unit: 50 troy ozs
Minimum purity: 99.8%
Prices in US dollars
Delivery: approved depository New York

Palladium

Palladium: world production, 1975 and 1976 *million troy ounces*

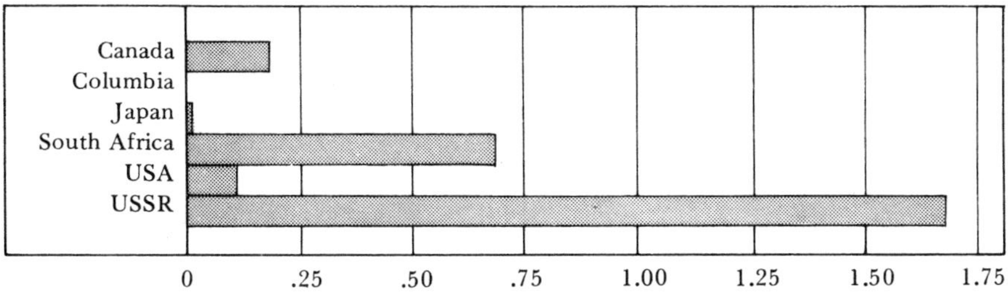

Reserves 177 million troy ounces *See Appendix 1, page 133*

Grades available

Palladium is priced and marketed in troy ounce units. The most commonly traded forms are ingot and sponge (irregular granules) but it is also made available by manufacturers and fabricators in the form of powder, rod, wire and even tube.

International dealers make only a hazy distinction between sponge and powder. There is no difference in price, unless a consumer needs a powder of a particular grain size, and the same material may be described by one dealer as sponge and by another as powder.

Ingots may weigh from 2.8 to 7.5 kilos, depending on the preference of the original producer.

The specification of minimum purity on most internationally traded contracts is 99.9 percent for both major forms of the metal, but actual purity is almost invariably higher at 99.95 percent or even 99.99 percent.

Many producers offer a range of palladium alloys.

Production method

Palladium is produced only as a by-product of platinum, which is itself associated with larger proportions of metals such as nickel, silver, gold and other metals in the platinum group.

After the removal of these precious metals by dissolving in aqua regia, the palladium is precipitated from the platinum-palladium salt solution by the addition of excess ammonium hydrochloride. The precipitate turns to palladium sponge when heated in a hydrogen atmosphere. The metal is melted in an inert crucible in an induction furnace then cast into graphite moulds.

Major uses

Palladium has properties in common with all the platinum group metals. It is almost totally corrosion-free and is most often used in alloy form with other precious metals. Its main applications are in electronics as electrical contacts, particularly in telephone systems, and as resistance windings especially where high precision is required.

Gold palladium alloys are used as electrothermal fuses, particularly in electric furnaces. Gold palladium and other palladium alloys are used in certain types of thermocouples, and palladium itself has a wide use as a catalyst for the production of, among other things, ethylene and vitamins A and E. It is also used for welding, particularly for jewellery; in dentistry; and as a palladium silver alloy for brazing stainless steel. Palladium is alloyed in small quantities with other precious metals, particularly platinum, for making jewellery, especially for setting precious stones.

Main market features

Palladium is the second most important platinum group metal, after platinum itself, both in terms of the quantity produced and in its industrial role. It differs from platinum, gold and silver in that its market is controlled almost entirely by the normal forces of industrial supply and demand and has therefore almost no monetary element. In this respect it resembles the non-precious metals.

Palladium production is almost as large as that of platinum but not as important industrially. All platinum group metals are found in association with each other in the same ore, often the ore of another metal such as gold or nickel. The Soviet Union produces about twice as much palladium as it does platinum and is by far the largest producer of the metal.

The ore in which the Russian palladium is found contains nickel, which is a co-product. This has an important bearing on the palladium market, as in periods when the nickel price is low the production of platinum group metals is more costly and may even be curtailed.

The price of nickel rose in early 1979 after having been extremely low in the previous three years. This has been suggested as the reason for the diminished level of Russian sales of all platinum group metals over this period.

Palladium consumption, 1974

troy ounces x 1000

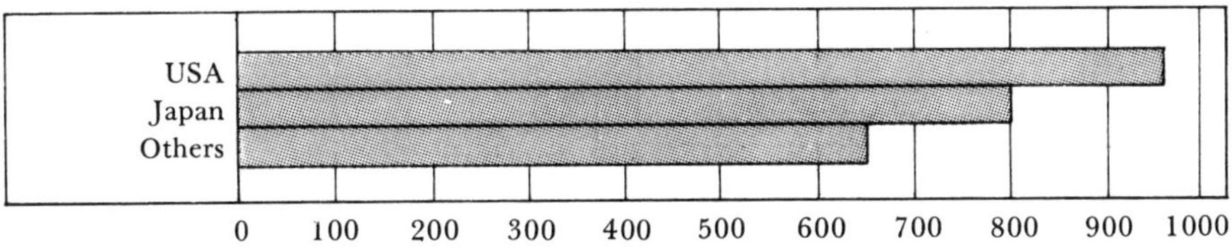

See Appendix 1, page 133

Palladium consumption by uses in US, 1976

	troy ounces x 1000
Automotive	194
Chemical	135
Petroleum	8
Glass	3
Electrical	160
Dental/Medical	150
Jewellery/Decorative	15
Miscellaneous & undistributed	60
Total	725

Source: American Bureau of Metal Statistics Inc

The Soviet Union does not normally withdraw completely from the market when it wishes to curtail sales; instead it prices itself out of the market by offering metal at some five dollars per troy ounce above the market price. The dual result of this policy is to sell less metal and to help raise the price: a very satisfactory situation as far as the Russians are concerned.

The market is made by a very small number of traders and banks in America, Europe and Japan. They buy from the Soviet Union, Canada and South Africa and sell to consumers. They also deal actively between themselves. Deals are most commonly on the scale of 500 to 1,000 ounces.

Producers themselves often take advantage of the market and may well buy large quantities, often before raising the so-called 'producer price'. The producer price is used as a basis for long-term contracts and for pricing fabricated items. In effect it follows the movements of the free market fairly closely.

An investor who wishes to buy palladium would find it almost impossible to buy directly from a producer at the producer price if the free market price was higher. It would be necessary to approach free market dealers to obtain supplies.

Much palladium is used in the form of alloys with platinum and other metals. This means that if a high palladium-containing platinum alloy is recommended for a new use the demand for palladium may rise disproportionately to the demand for platinum and vice versa. Palladium is particularly important in the production of catalytic converters in motor and car exhaust systems and anti-pollution legislation in the United States may specify a high palladium-containing alloy for this purpose.

Japan is an extremely important consumer of palladium, where it is mainly alloyed with platinum or gold for the manufacture of jewellery.

Palladium prices: annual average, 1968-1978 (producer price)

US dollars/troy ounce

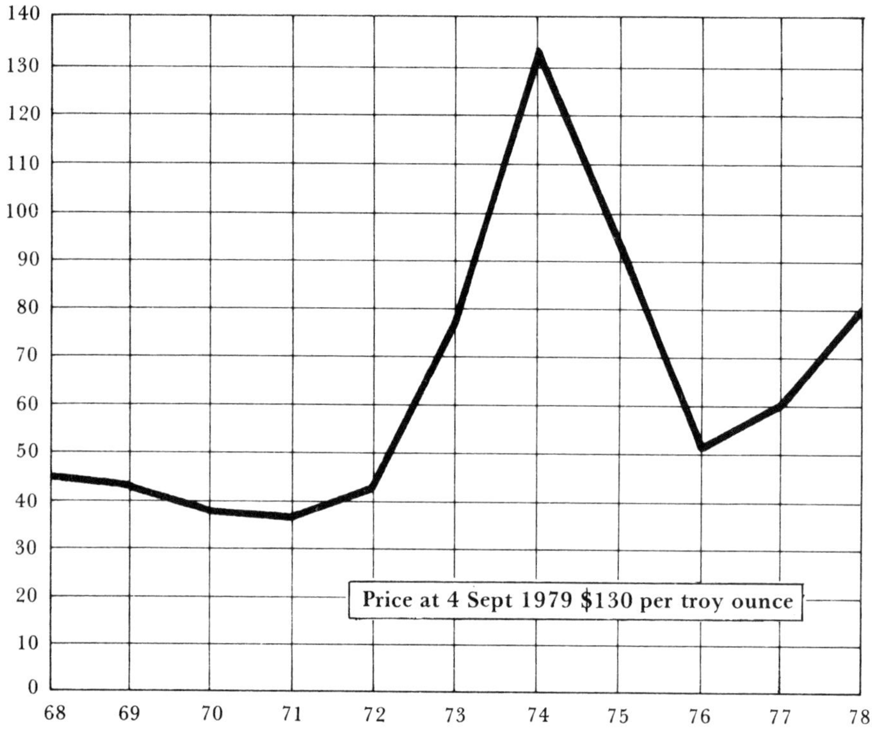

See Appendix 1, page 133

Source: Metal Bulletin

Palladium trading: market

NEW YORK MERCANTILE EXCHANGE
4 World Trade Center
New York
NY 10048
Tel. 212 938 2222

Chief Executive: Richard B. Levine
Palladium trading each weekday:
10-20 – 13.30 eastern standard time

Trading unit: 100 troy ozs
Minimum purity: 99.8%
Prices: in US dollars
Delivery: approved depository New York

Rhodium

Rhodium: world production, 1975 *troy ounces x 1000*

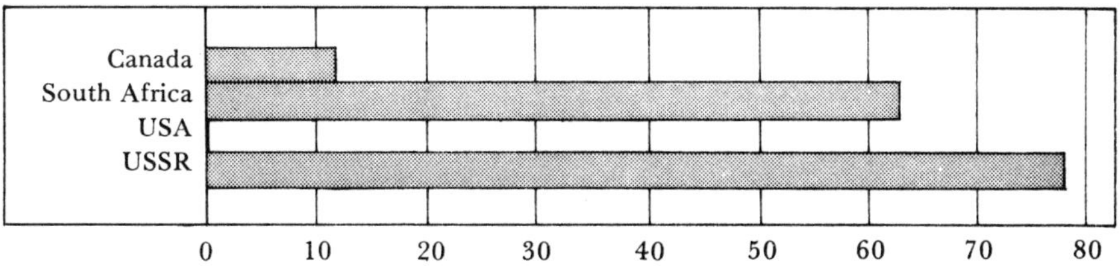

Reserves 5.28 million ounces *See Appendix 1, page 133*

Grades available

Like other precious metals, rhodium is traded in units of troy ounces. Although some producers offer the metal in the form of bars, almost all international trading is in the form of sponge or powder with a minimum purity of 99.9 percent. The purity of most of the metal traded is higher at 99.95 percent.

Production method

Rhodium, too, is a by-product of platinum production. After the platinum has been removed by dissolving in aqua regia, the residue is decomposed with iron and warmed with concentrated nitric acid. It is then heated with potash, after which the residue is mixed with salt and heated in chlorine, which converts the iridium to iridum chloride when treated with nitric acid and precipitated with ammonium chloride, leaving rhodium ammonium-chloride in solution. Rhodium metal powder is produced on heating. This can be converted to solid bars by sintering.

Major uses

This metal has an extremely high resistance to corrosion and it is used to plate steel and brass and many other metals in order to prevent corrosion from sea water and other elements. In these instances the rhodium coating is extremely thin and used only when the cost is justified.

As an alloy with platinum (containing about 10 percent rhodium) it has many uses as spinerettes in man-made fibre production, in thermocouples, for windings in electric furnaces and in other electrical equipment. This alloy's most significant use is as a catalyst in the production of nitric acid from ammonia, where it is used in the form of a fine gauze. The metal has several other important catalytic uses.

An interesting physical characteristic of rhodium is its very high optical reflectivity, which is particularly useful since it is an almost untarnishable metal. This quality has given rhodium many applications in optical equipment where the metal is deposited in extremely thin layers on optically ground surfaces.

On occasions rhodium is alloyed with gold, platinum and other metals for use in jewellery.

Main market features

Rhodium is now the most expensive of all precious metals. Its high value is determined almost exclusively by its industrial usefulness rather than by virtue of any monetary component in the market.

Most rhodium is used as a minor addition to precious metal alloys. As with the other more obscure platinum group metals, demand fluctuates if the rhodium content in one of these alloys is increased to accommodate a new use. Rhodium is one of the metals under consideration for the manufacture of the 'three way' catalytic converter which may be included in the exhaust systems of motor cars in the United States in order to limit harmful fumes. If this happens, the demand for rhodium may increase to the point where its proportion in the alloy used is greater than its proportion in the platinum ore from which it is refined. This means that if the ore contains 60 percent platinum and five percent rhodium – as a proportion of the total platinum group metal content – and the main alloy used contains 85 percent platinum and 15 percent rhodium, supplies of rhodium will run out eventually unless platinum production rises. Since rhodium forms such a small proportion of most platinum ores, this is unlikely.

The data on the proportion of rhodium produced as a percentage of platinum produced are only estimates, as it has proved impossible to obtain precise figures. Some experts put the rhodium content in Russian ore as high as 10 percent, others as low as two percent of total platinum group metal content. In any case this proportion may vary from year to year. Any assumptions concerning future supply are therefore extremely difficult to make.

The Japanese are frequently heavy buyers of rhodium for use as an alloy in jewellery and they may, on occasions, buy up all available supplies on the free market.

The Soviet Union, which has an unpredictable sales policy, has in recent months all but withdrawn from the market.

As with the other lesser known precious metals, the rhodium market consists of a handful of specialist traders around the world who do as much trading with each other as they do with producers and consumers. The average deal between such traders is about 100 troy ounces.

The market is generally unpredictable and in times of rapid movement it may be difficult for an outsider to trade at market levels. It is therefore not recommended as an investment item, unless the investor is prepared to spend time studying the mechanics of the market.

Rhodium prices: annual average, 1968-1978 (producer price)

US dollars/troy ounce

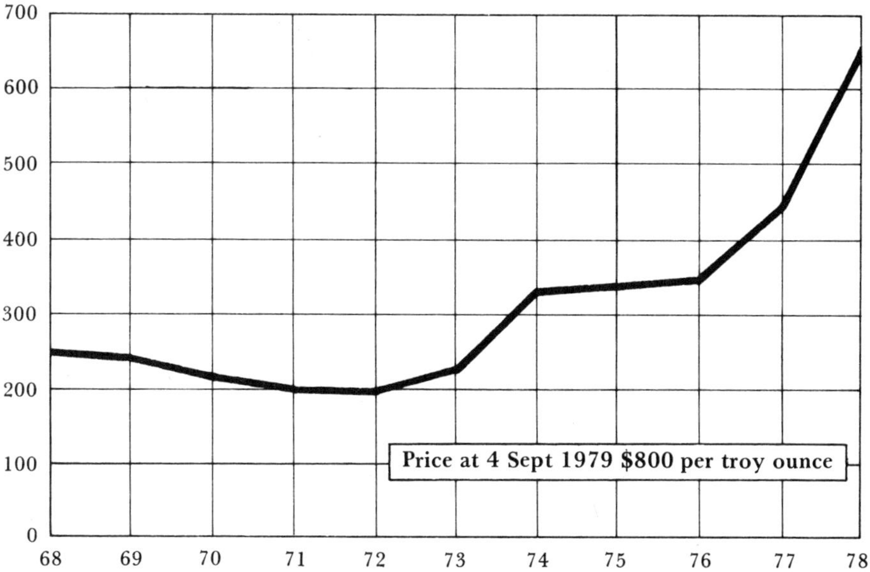

See Appendix 1, page 134 *Source: Metal Bulletin*

Iridium

Iridium: world production, 1975

troy ounces x 1000

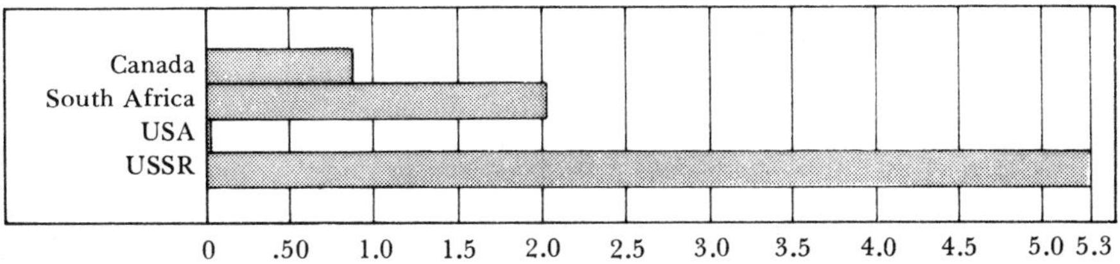

Reserves 5.91 million ounces

See Appendix 1, page 134

Grades available

Iridium is not as popular with traders as is platinum or palladium. It is usually sold in troy ounce units in the form of powder or, far less commonly, as ingots with a purity of 99.9 percent minimum.

Production method

The metal is produced as a by-product of platinum production. Unlike platinum it does not dissolve in aqua regia and is separated from platinum by treatment with this substance in metal and salt form. It can be separated from osmium by oxidizing the osmium.

Iridium is melted in a thoria crucible in a high frequency electric furnace and poured into moulds. It is brittle at room temperature and cannot be worked except at white heat.

Major uses

Iridium is a hard and brittle metal and difficult to work mechanically. It is used usually in the form of an alloy with platinum in which the iridium constitutes less than 20 percent. This alloy is used for electrical contacts, particularly when these have to be robust. It is also used in jewellery, especially for setting diamonds.

Its alloy with ruthenium and with osmium (osmium iridium alloys

Iridium prices: annual average, 1968-78 (producer price)
US dollars/troy ounce

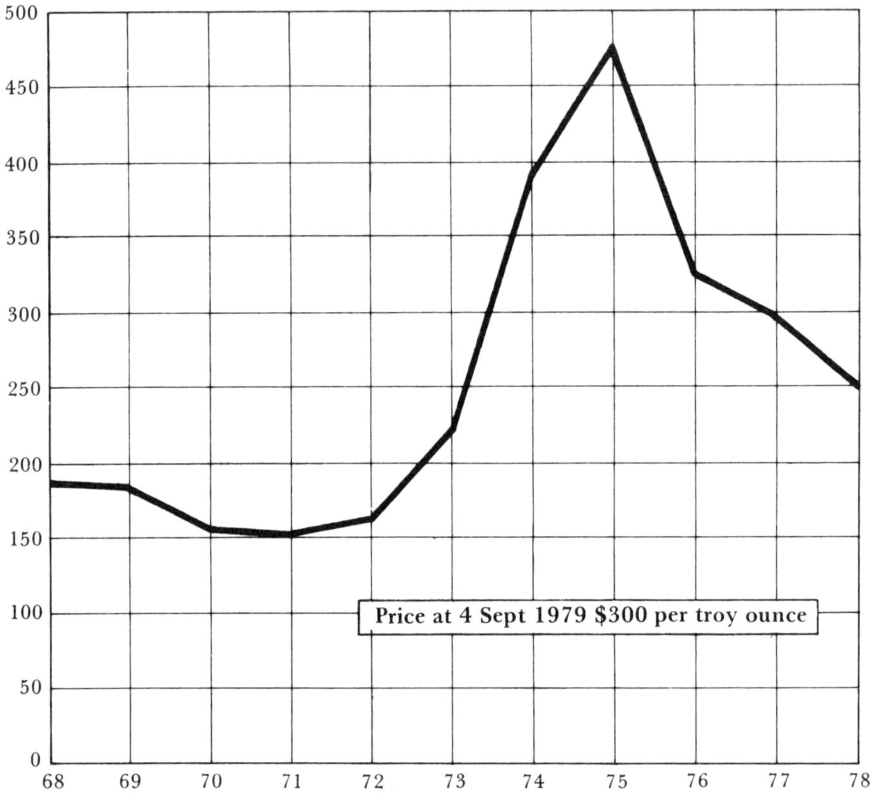

See Appendix 1, page 134

are known as osmiridium) are used extensively for making the tips of fountain pen nibs. This is usually done by powder metallurgy, ie by mixing the powders of the two metals to the right proportions, then fusing them in the mould required.

The metal can be used in sensitive equipment where contact with mercury is necessary, as iridium is not 'wetted' by the liquid metal.

Its alloy with platinum is used in precision resistance wiring.

The metal is also used to make crucibles and other laboratory equipment for high temperature work (its melting point is 2454°C), as it is the most corrosion-resistant of all elements.

Main market features

The iridium market is small and traded by only a few precious metal merchants. Its uses are not as important as those for platinum and palladium. Iridium is an extremely expensive metal and is used mainly as a minor addition in precious metal alloys.

In 1979 the USSR became a reluctant seller of iridium and other platinum group metals. This suggests that the Russians are either producing only enough for their own requirements or that they do not regard the price as sufficiently high and therefore do not wish to increase sales. This policy may change if nickel prices increase, as most Russian platinum group metals are found in association with nickel ores. Canada and South Africa are the main suppliers to the market at present.

Iridium is cheaper than both platinum and rhodium and, for this reason, is likely to be the most popular alloy addition in platinum jewellery, most of which is produced by Japan.

The market is so thin at times that any large purchase of a few hundred ounces could increase the market price by five or 10 dollars per ounce.

Iridium prices are not much affected by changes in the price of other platinum group metals. However, as it is a by-product of platinum refining, production will fall if platinum production falls.

Osmium

Osmium: world production, 1975 *troy ounces*

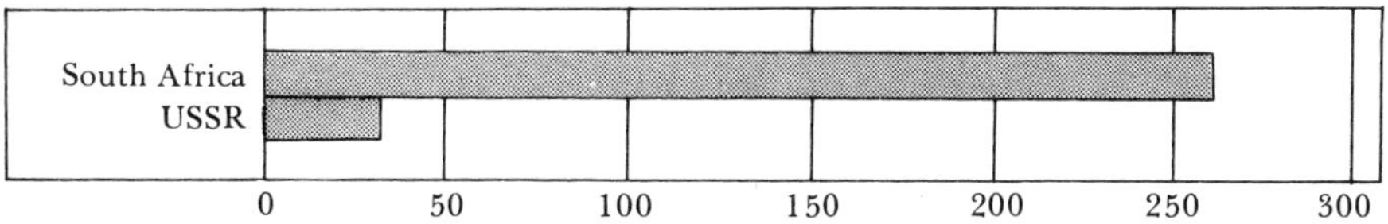

Reserves 20,000 ounces *See Appendix 1, page 134*

Grades available

Osmium is only rarely traded on an open market but is made available in the form of sponge with a purity of 99.5 percent minimum or 99.9 percent minimum. It is traded and priced in units of troy ounces.

Production method

Osmium is produced as a by-product of platinum production and is naturally associated with iridium; this combination is known as osmiridium. It is separated from platinum by the same method used to extract iridium.

The sulphide is heated in a crucible then heated with tin and charcoal. The tin is then dissolved with hydrochloric acid and the pure metal obtained by heating the residue in hydrogen.

Major uses

Osmium is extremely hard and heavy. Unlike most precious metals, however, it oxidizes quite easily in air at 130°C, giving off poisonous fumes.

Its hardness has found applications, particularly in alloy form, for fountain pen nibs, spindle pivots and as electrical contacts. It also has some application as a catalyst but none of its uses are of particular importance.

Main market features

Osmium is one of the least significant of the precious metals. As with all the platinum group metals, it is used mainly in highly sophisticated areas of industry and may yet be of significance; its hardness particularly may find important applications.

The market is so small that if such an application is found supplies would be very limited. Osmium constitutes only a minute proportion of all the platinum group metals found in the common ore, which itself is an infinitesimal proportion of the minerals in which it is found.

Most current applications for osmium are as an alloy addition to other precious metals, particularly in osmiridium, an alloy of osmium and iridium. This alloy is produced directly from the ore, without the two constituent metals being separated in the refining process.

Even the merchants who specialize in trading precious metals rarely trade osmium. Most consumers rely on supplies from the major producers, particularly South Africa.

Production statistics are difficult to obtain as most producers tend to give one figure reflecting the total production of all the rarer platinum group metals.

Osmium prices: annual average, 1968-1978 (producer price)

US dollars/troy ounce

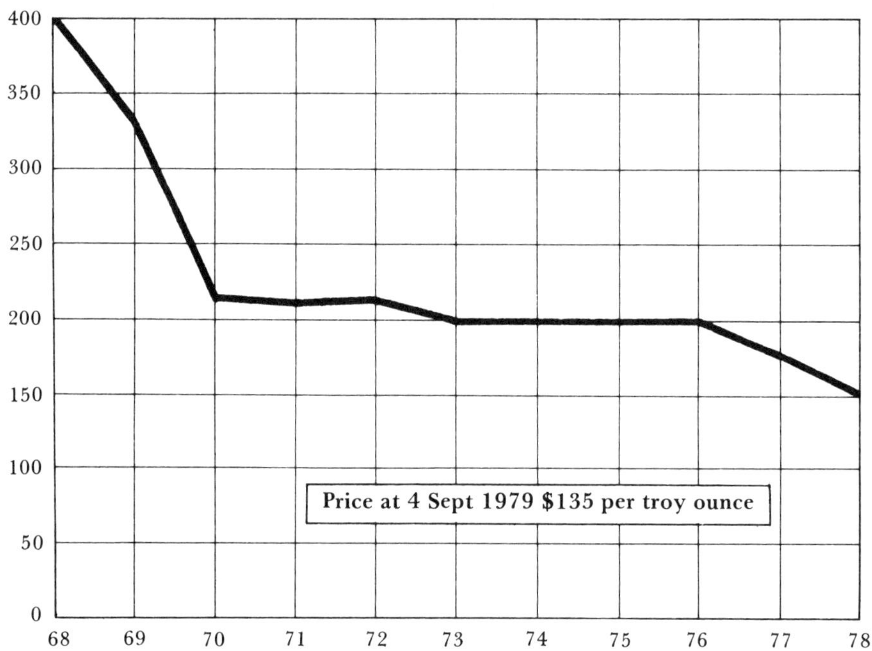

See Appendix 1, page 135

Source: Metal Bulletin

Ruthenium

Ruthenium: world production, 1975 *troy ounces x 1000*

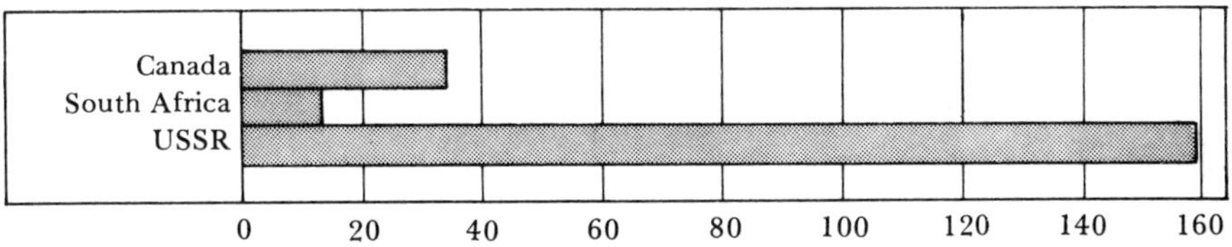

Approx Reserves 14.36 million ounces *See Appendix 1, page 135*

Grades available

Like other precious metals ruthenium is traded in troy ounces. Almost all of it is used for alloying with other metals using a powder metallurgy technique and therefore the bulk of ruthenium is traded in the form of powder with a minimum purity of 99.9 percent.

Production method

Ruthenium is also a platinum group metal and is separated from other platinum metals as a volatile tetroxide. It is then dissolved in dilute hydrochloric acid containing methyl alcohol. When evaporated, an oxychloride is produced and the pure metal can be obtained by reaction of this compound with hydrogen.

Major uses

Ruthenium's principal uses are as an alloy with platinum containing between 10 and 15 percent ruthenium. In this form it is used for jewellery and for electrical contacts.

It is also used as a catalyst in the manufacture of paraffin wax but outside this product its catalytic uses are limited.

Main market features

Ruthenium is the cheapest of all the platinum group metals, owing more to its inessential uses than to its scarcity, since it is one of the rarest elements known.

Like osmium, it is seldom traded and the market is, in many cases, very small. A 200 ounce order for the metal would be considered substantial.

The producers most prepared to offer ruthenium to dealers are Canadians. The South Africans sell directly to consumers and the Russians rarely export the metal.

It is possible that a more important use may be found for ruthenium: its properties could be exploited for gas absorption. However, as with osmium, supplies are so limited that anyone considering its use on a larger scale would have to take serious account of the effect that any increase in demand would have on its price.

The cheapness of the metal compared with the other precious metals may make it more popular as an alloy addition to platinum in jewellery, and in areas where it can be substituted for these metals, such as in electronics.

Ruthenium prices: annual average, 1968-1978 (producer price)

US dollars/troy ounce

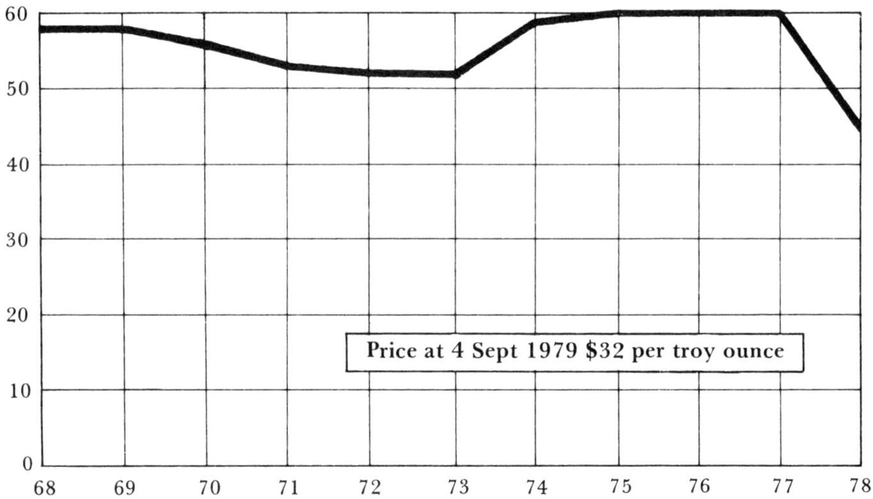

See Appendix 1, page 135

Source: Metal Bulletin

Methods of trading platinum, palladium and other platinum group metals

Platinum, palladium and the other platinum group metals, are marketed in two separate ways. The bulk of supplies are sold by the mining companies, via marketing agents, to consumers at a published producer price used in supply contracts. This is the system used by Western world producers, led by South Africa, for channelling a regular flow of supplies to consumers at a known price. Producers adjust their selling prices according to market conditions and developments, but it is the producer who makes the decision though the views of buyers might be a major influence.

There is also the so-called 'free market', used by Communist bloc countries and other sources of supply, to channel sales to consumers, mainly via specialist merchants. The supplies, sold via the free market, come from a variety of different sources.

In the case of platinum and palladium the Soviet Union is normally the major supplier to the free market. Other sources include consumers selling surplus holdings; minor producers and investment stocks, held by both trade and private speculators as well as financial institutions. Merchants on occasions also build up stocks, generally bought from Western producers, that are resold on the free market.

Free market prices fluctuate constantly in line with supply and demand developments. They provide a more topical indication of current trends than does the fixed producer price, ie, whether there is a shortage, surplus, or evenly balanced supply/demand situation.

However, the free market, if starved of supplies or swamped with a surplus, can be artificially distorted and manipulated to exaggerate either an upward or downward trend. For example, there may be an acute shortage of supplies available to the free market forcing prices higher and higher, while the bulk of demand is still being satisfied by producers supplying consumers direct with their requirements under the producer price system. The free market prices, inflated by shortage, do not therefore represent the true overall situation.

The percentage of total sales going through the free market varies according to circumstances. In times of an overall shortage of supplies to meet the demand, the amount sold via the free market may be substantially reduced, as consumers hold on to their stocks and producers have difficulty in meeting their contractual supply commitments. Conversely, in times of surplus, producers may be keen to offload extra supplies on the free market and consumers may be anxious to reduce their stocks by free market sales.

The shifting pattern of supply and demand is reflected, and often anticipated, by movements in free market prices. The futures markets for platinum and palladium in the United States are a comparatively new addition to the free market system. The basic function of these futures markets is to offer protection for producers, consumers and merchants against price fluctuations by providing hedging facilities: physical transactions are matched by an opposite transaction on the futures market, so that whichever way prices move the loss and profit made on either market cancel each other out.

However, where the bulk of supplies is sold at a fixed producer price, there is little need for hedging. The main role of the platinum and palladium futures markets is to provide a central pricing medium reflecting all the influences, including most importantly, speculative forces. In recent years, aided by the futures market, speculative interest in platinum as an alternative to gold and silver has increased enormously.

The attraction of platinum as an investment is that it tends to move in line with gold. Both metals come from similar sources – South Africa and the Soviet Union; both are rare and therefore precious metals; and gold and platinum are interchangeable in certain uses, notably jewellery and electronics.

At the same time they are both easy to store, taking up relatively little space. However, many speculators, not wishing to lock their money away in an investment which produces no dividend or interest, prefer to deal in paper futures where they have only to put up a margin.

Both the platinum and palladium futures markets are on the New York Mercantile Exchange, nowadays housed with the other commodity futures markets at the World Trade Center. So far a platinum futures contract in Chicago has failed to attract much support but there are plans for the launching of a new market on the Chicago Mercantile Exchange.

In New York the platinum futures contract has been particularly successful in attracting considerable support and in influencing price movements in London and the rest of the world. Although physical trading via the futures market is very small, especially in the case of palladium, the movement of prices is important since it represents a trend decided in open trading with commitments from both buyers and sellers.

In London the marketing of platinum has historically been linked with that of gold, mainly because they both come from similar sources in South Africa.

The selling agent for Rustenburg Platinum Mines, the biggest single platinum producer, is Johnson Matthey, who are also bullion brokers as well as being refiners of precious metals. Inevitably this has meant that the bulk of platinum group metal sales go through the bullion brokers, who deal in other precious metals as well. In recent years, as interest in platinum group metals has increased, the number of dealers involved has grown. Three companies in London – Ayrton Metals, a subsidiary of Impala Platinum Mines, the second biggest South African producer; Argos Metals; and bullion brokers Samuel Montagu decided they should agree a market price for platinum twice a day – once in the morning and once in the afternoon. This is a similar arrangement to the gold and silver 'fixings' held by the London bullion brokers, although the companies concerned claim it is rather different. The formula, however, is the same. The three participants contact each other to work out a price at which they are prepared to do business – either to buy or to sell – at a particular time. Obviously the trend in the New York futures market is taken into account, as well as the many orders from clients. The price agreed tends to reflect the day-to-day demand for physical supplies, but the companies concerned, as well as many other commodity brokers, do deal with orders for future deliveries as well and it is hoped, eventually, that a platinum futures market will be launched in London. Meanwhile the official quotations of free market platinum prices, on a daily basis, are used as a formula for pricing on long-term forward supply contracts.

A significant development in recent years has been the growing influence of the free market over the producer price system. At one time platinum producers tended to ignore developments in the free market, since it was considered to be relatively unimportant. But the situation has changed with the tremendous surge of interest from investors, who can only really buy platinum from free market sources as the producers are unwilling, and often unable, to meet small individual orders on an irregular basis. Producers have tapped the speculative market by the production of special ingots, tailored for the individual investor. But it is left to the free market to handle the huge accumulation of speculative funds that can build up at times. Producers have become very much more aware of the increasingly powerful forces at work in the free market, over and above the Russians, who can influence prices heavily either by increasing, or reducing, the amount of supplies channelled to the Western world, as is seen in the case of gold. In the case of palladium the Russians are particularly important as they are the dominant world producer.

Free market trading in the more specialized metals, such as iridium and rhodium, is much less important, though still a good indicator of underlying supply/demand trends. Platinum producers, in the past, have proved to be very poor forecasters of the future trend of demand. This has persuaded them to pay a great deal more attention to the free market and to change their producer prices much more frequently to coincide with developments in this market.

Consumption by uses of platinum group metals, 1976 (excluding platinum and palladium)

	troy ounces x 1000
Automotive	–
Chemical	15
Petroleum	2
Glass	5
Electrical	18
Dental and Medical	2
Jewellery and Decorative	15
Miscellaneous and Undistributed	15
Total	72

Source: American Bureau of Metal Statistics Inc

US stockpile at 31 May, 1978

troy ounces

	Inventory	Disposal	Objective
Iridium	16,990	–	97,761
Palladium	1,252,789	–	2,450,000
Platinum	439,599	–	1,314,000
Silver	139,500,000	139,500,000	–

Source: General Services Administration

Secondary sources of palladium, rhodium, iridium, osmium and ruthenium

The reclamation of the above Platinum Group Metals (PGM) is limited as their general use is only as a subordinate alloying agent with other metals. For instance in the United States in 1976 it was estimated that approximately 107,000 troy ounces of palladium, 1,500 troy ounces of iridium, and 6,500 troy ounces of other PGMs were recovered by refiners. This substantial recovery is due to the high value of the metals and the technical expertise of the refiners.

The secondary sources of PGM are the same as for the other precious metals – the electrical, jewellery, petroleum, chemical and dental industries. The material arises in the form of spent catalysts, clad materials, contact points, dental sweeps, jewellery scrap, paste, plated parts, electrical relays, sludges, chemicals, solutions, and wire.

Though these are high priced metals they are used usually in only limited proportions with platinum; silver or gold are the more dominant metals. It therefore may not be worthwhile to separate the PGMs from the rest and the alloy is simply refined and returned to the consumer. In these cases the refiner and merchant may not even attribute any value to or pay for the PGM content. There are attempts to use more PGMs and less platinum in, for instance, electronics or as catalysts, but the PGM must be a much larger percentage of the alloy before it can be considered an element that can be recycled.

Part 6: Metallurgy

Metallurgy

GOLD

Symbol:	Au
Atomic Number:	79
Atomic Weight:	197.2
Density:	At 20° C (68° F) is 19.32 g/cc (0.689 lb/cu in)
Melting point:	1062.8° C
Boiling Point:	2360° C
Electrical Resistivity:	2.3 micro Ohm-cms at 20° C (68° F)

IRIDIUM

Symbol:	Ir
Atomic Number:	77
Atomic Weight:	193.1
Density:	At 20° C (68° F) 22.5 gr/cc (0.813 lb/cu in)
Melting Point:	2454 ± 3° C (4449 ± 5° F)
Boiling Point:	5300° C (9570° F)
Electrical Resistivity:	5.3 micro-Ohms-cms at 20° C (68° F)
Other Properties:	Brittle at room temperature, malleable at white heat. Most corrosion resistant of all the elements and resistant to most ordinary acids. Alloyed mainly with platinum to give hardness.

OSMIUM

Symbol:	Os
Atomic Number:	76
Atomic Weight:	190.2
Density:	At 20° C (68° F) 22.57g/cc (0.8154lb/cu in)
Melting Point:	2700 ± 200° C (4900 ± 350° F)
Boiling Point:	5500° C (9950° F)
Electrical Resistivity:	9.5 micro Ohm-cms at 20° C (68° F)
Other Properties:	Brittle, heaviest metal, when oxidized gives off toxic fumes

PALLADIUM

Symbol:	Pd
Atomic Number:	46
Atomic Weight:	106.7
Density:	At 20° C (68° F) 12.02 g/cc (0.4343lb/cu in)
Melting Point:	1552° C (2826° F)
Boiling Point:	3989° C (7200° F)
Electrical Resistivity:	10.8 micro Ohm-cms at 20° C (68° F)
Other Properties:	Very malleable and ductile

PLATINUM

Symbol:	Pt
Atomic Number:	78
Atomic Weight:	195.23
Density:	At 20° C (68° F) 21.5 g/cc (0.7772lb/cu in)
Melting Point:	1773.5° C
Boiling Point:	4300° C
Electrical Resistivity:	10.6 micro Ohm-cms at 20° C (68° F)

RHODIUM

Symbol:	Rh
Atomic Number:	45
Atomic Weight:	102.91
Density:	At 20° C (68° F) 12.44 g/cc (0.447 lb/cu in)
Melting Point:	1966 ± 3° C (3571 ± 5° F)
Boiling Point:	4500° C (8130° F)
Electrical Resistivity:	4.7 micro Ohm-cms at 20° C (68° F)
Other Properties:	Unattacked in normal atmosphere, high resistance to corrosion

RUTHENIUM

Symbol:	Ru
Atomic Number:	44
Atomic Weight:	101.7
Density:	At 20° C (68° F) 12.2 g/cc (0.441lb/cu in)
Melting Point:	2500 ± 100° C (4530 ± 180° F)
Boiling Point:	4900° C (8850° F)
Electrical Resistivity:	7.3 micro Ohm-cms at 20° C (68° F)
Other Properties:	High corrosion resistant, brittle

SILVER

Symbol:	Ag
Atomic Number:	47
Atomic Weight:	101.88
Density:	At 20°C (68°F) 10.5 g/cc (0.3791lb/cu in)
Melting Point:	960.5°C
Boiling Point:	2152°C
Electrical Resistivity:	1.6 micro Ohm-cms at 20°C (68°F)

Recent developments

During the late summer of 1979, at the time of this book going to print, prices of the most important precious metals, gold, silver and platinum, rose to unprecedented high levels.

Such rises were a direct consequence of widely held doubts concerning the value of the weaker currencies, and to the political developments in Iran. Much of the buying interest in gold has come from the Arab world and from private citizens in the United States and the Far East. The parallel rise in the price of silver and platinum emphasizes the traditional link, in the minds of investors, between the markets of these metals. Changes in supply and industrial demand are minor and cannot therefore be considered as an explanation for these price movements.

The buying interest in precious metals is taking place against an economic background which is a contradiction of traditional economic theory in that recession and inflation are occurring simultaneously. This is termed 'stagflation'.

It would be dogmatic to suggest that any market which increases by 1000 percent in a decade is unstable, and gold is certainly a special case. However, it has been pointed out elsewhere in this book that, as gold no longer fulfils a monetary role, its market is subject to the normal rules of supply and demand, excepting only that gold has been historically regarded as a hedge against inflation and other forms of economic dislocation. The faith that gold buyers have in its ability to fulfil this role is likely to be sorely tested in the immediate future. A similar price rise in any other commodity would be considered freakish and extremely dangerous.

It is difficult to make a precise analysis of the type of people who have invested in gold in recent years but many experts agree that a disproportionate number have based their actions on inadequate reasoning reinforced by the media. If the more substantial investment institutions decide to take advantage of the profits they have made – which would reduce price levels – the resultant wave of selling is likely to assume panic proportions. And the consequent large drop in price would completely undermine the small investor's faith in gold for some time.

However, there are strong arguments to support the view that, while there are so few investment opportunities available in a period of recession, gold will maintain its high price levels.

Most of the world's silver and platinum are used industrially and in a period of economic decline requirements will diminish. An obvious concern to platinum producers is that fewer cars will be produced in the United States and those that are produced will be smaller in size, thus reducing consumption in catalytic converters.

Present trends indicate that the material displaced by a lack of industrial demand will be taken up by investors but this will depend on the severity of the depression and the behaviour of the gold market.

The higher the price of gold, the more risky investment in gold becomes. If, for instance, an investor has the alternative investment yielding a 13 percent return, which is possible in a period of high interest rates, the price of gold would need to rise from say $320 to $362 in order to compete. At the same time investors should avoid the temptation of 'going short' ie selling gold with the expectation of buying it later at a lower price.

The behaviour of the gold market may be unpredictable at the present high levels.

Between early January and early September 1979 the percentage rise in the price of precious metals was approximately as follows:

Precious metal	*Percentage price rise*
gold	38
silver	57
platinum	15
palladium	62
rhodium	23

Other platinum group metals have shown only small price changes with some falls in price over this period.

Platinum has not performed as well as the other metals mainly because of the fear of a drop in consumption by the automobile industry. These fears, however, have not affected the palladium price. The difference in behaviour of these two markets is probably attributable to the continuing lack of supplies from the Soviet Union, which used to supply a greater proportion of palladium than platinum; and to the large difference between their prices.

Also in the period January to September 1979 the prices of most industrial metals such as copper, lead, nickel and aluminium have shown slight rises of the order of a few percent, demonstrating that, although inflation has been on the increase worldwide, the recession in industrial activity has not, as yet, affected demand sufficiently to lower prices.

There is no doubt that the economic situation in the United States is deteriorating: with inflation above 11 percent; unemployment above six percent; most of the important decisions concerning the conservation of energy still to be taken; and the effects of the disruption of oil supplies from Iran creating critical problems.

American industry consumes such a large proportion of the world's metals that any decline in industrial activity in the United States has a considerable effect on metal prices. At the time of writing it is too early to say whether the US administration will attempt to squeeze inflation out of the economy by reducing money supply or whether, in election year, President Carter will bow to pressures from some quarters to reduce taxes in order to stimulate the economy. The latter option will have the effect of slowing down the rate of increase in unemployment but will stimulate inflation and the consumption of metals. It will also, almost certainly, have the effect of helping to keep precious metal prices strong. If, on the other hand, the world is moving into a period where governments make a concerted effort to ignore short-term pressures to relieve the unemployment situation in order to bring inflation under control, there can be little expectation of precious metal prices rising much further, and they may well drop dramatically.

A further important consideration, which must be stressed as these metals advance in price, is the certainty that some precious metals may be becoming too expensive and that, in consequence, demand in certain areas will fall. Investigations into the substitution of these metals in industry is stimulated by higher prices and although the markets of these metals have so far displayed remarkable elasticity in the face of rising prices, the point must come where many potential buyers of, say, jewellery are priced out of the market or must settle for lower purity items. After all, only an expert could tell the difference between a nine carat and an 18 carat ring.

It is clear that there is still a vast pool of money available to be invested in this type of speculative venture. As the price of the metals rises and becomes more speculative, these funds spill over into other associated investments such as gold shares, other precious metals and the shares of the companies which mine these metals. The effect of high prices and investment in shares must stimulate higher production.

British legislation, October 1979

The Conservative Government repealed all restrictions covering the trading of gold between private citizens. Purchases of gold, however, remain subject to a VAT levy of 15 per cent.

Appendices

Appendix 1:

Tables

Gold production: world total, 1968-1977

Year	*metric tons*	Year	*metric tons*	Year	*metric tons*
1968	1567.6	1972	1530.0	1976	1435.0
1969	1588.7	1973	1539.3	1977	1428.5
1970	1638.7	1974	1449.5		
1971	1613.8	1975	1384.1		

Source: Metal Bulletin

Gold production by country, 1977

Country	*metric tons*
South Africa	699.9
Canada	54.3
USA	32.5
Rhodesia	20.0
Ghana	16.9
Zaire	3.0
Other	1.0
Total other Africa	40.9
Brazil	12.9
Dominican Rep	10.5
Columbia	9.2
Mexico	6.7
Peru	3.4
Nicaragua	2.0
Other	8.0
Total Latin America	52.7
Philippines	18.5
Japan	4.7
India	2.5
Other	3.0
Total Asia	28.7
Total Europe	11.0

Gold production by country, 1977 (cont'd)

Country	*metric tons*
Papua/New Guinea	22.3
Australia	19.2
Other	3.0
Total Oceania	44.5
Total non-communist world	964.5
USSR (est)	444.0
Other communist countries	20.0
World total	1428.5

Source: Consolidated Goldfields

Gold mines in South Africa: production costs based on fourth quarter returns, December 1978

Mine	*US dollars/troy ounces*
East Driefontein	49.69
West Driefontein	52.82
Winkelhaak	76.26
Kloof	82.90
St Helena	88.84
Western Holdings	89.13
F S Geduld	89.18
W Deep Levels	92.08
Randfontein	98.08
Kinross	102.19
Pres Brand	102.37
Bracken	103.04
Marievale	106.04
Blyvoor	110.48
E T Cons	114.40
Hartebeest	119.07
Libanon	123.04
Grootvlei	132.76
Vaal Reefs	133.70
Doornfontein	136.60
Vlakfontein	138.51
Buffelsfontein	146.27
Pres Steyn	147.26
Leslie	151.35
Welkom	159.11
Western Areas	161.18
Stilfontein	164.04
Durban R Deep	194.68
Venterspost	194.74
F S Saaiplaas	234.01
ERPM	238.88
Loraine	256.61
W R Cons	509.60
Harmony	N/A

Source: Consolidated Goldfields

Gold bullion holdings by world governments, January 1978 (under Special Drawing Rights)

	million troy ounces
Industrial countries	
Austria	21.0
Belgium	42.4
Canada	22.0
Denmark	1.9
France	101.6
Germany	118.2
Italy	82.9
Japan	23.7
Netherlands	54.6
Norway	1.1
Sweden	5.9
Switzerland	83.3
UK	22.2
USA	277.5
Other Europe	
Finland	0.9
Greece	3.7
Ireland	0.5
Portugal	27.7
Spain	14.4
Turkey	3.6
Yugoslavia	1.5
Others	
Australia	7.7
New Zealand	0.06
South Africa	9.6
Oil exporters	
Algeria	5.5
Indonesia	0.2
Iran	3.8
Iraq	4.1
Kuwait	2.5
Libya	2.5
Nigeria	0.7
Saudi Arabia	3.1
UAE	0.6
Venezuela	11.3
Others	
Argentina	4.2
Bahrain	0.1
Brazil	1.5
Chile	1.3
China	2.4
Colombia	1.8
Dominican Republic	0.1
Ecuador	0.4
Egypt	2.4
El Salvador	0.5
Ethiopia	0.3
Ghana	0.2
Guatemala	0.5
India	1.8

Gold production by company, 1976 (cont'd)

Others (cont'd)	*million troy ounces*
Israel	1.2
Jordan	0.8
Korea	0.1
Lebanon	9.2
Malaysia	1.7
Mexico	1.7
Morocco	0.6
Netherland Antilles	0.5
Pakistan	1.7
Peru	1.0
Philippines	1.1
Thailand	2.4
Tunisia	0.2
Uruguay	3.6
Zaire	0.2
Total	1015.428

Gold production by company, 1976

Company	*troy ounces*
The Anaconda Company (own mines)	20,193
The Anaconda Company, Canada	–
Asarco Incorporated (own mines)	45,402
Ashanti: Goldfields Corp (Ghana) Ltd	372,689
Benquet Consolidated Inc, Philippines	111,861
Blyvooruitzicht, Transvaal, Inc, S Africa	748,119
Bolidens, Sweden	147,700
Buffelsfontein, Transvaal, S Africa	945,518
Bulolo, New Guinea	1,867
Cananea, Mexico	9,973
City Deep, Transvaal, S Africa	93,816
Codelco, Chile	
Division Chuquicamata	14,717
Division Salvador	13,621
Division El Tenieute	3,582
Consolidated Main Reef, Transvaal, S Africa	(included with City Deep)
Consolidated Rambler Mines Ltd, Canada	10,828
Cortez Gold Mine, USA	25,533
Crown Mines, Transvaal, S Africa	(included with City Deep)
Dome, Canada	119,504
Doornfontein, Transvaal, S Africa	387,641
Durban Roodeport Deep, Transvaal, S Africa	255,123
East Daggafontein, Transvaal, S Africa	69,809
East Rand Pty, Transvaal, S Africa	354,639
Freddies Consolidated, Orange Free State, S Africa	183,388
Free State Geduld, Orange Free State, S Africa	1,115,746
Grootvlei, Transvaal, S Africa	180,282
Harmony, Orange Free State, S Africa	976,482
Hartebeestfontein, Transvaal, S Africa	1,035,794
Heclan, USA	1,847
Hollinger, Canada	5,477
Homestake, USA	318,487
Hudson Bay, Canada	65,734
Industrial Minera Mexico SA, Mexico	44,506
Kalgoorie Lake View Pty Ltd, Australia	135,800
Kennscott Copper Corp, USA	237,260
Kerr-Addison, Canada	110,740
Kilo-Moto, Zaire	N/A
Lamaque, Canada	62,157
Libanon, Transvaal, S Africa	330,789
Loraine, Orange Free State, S Africa	253,878
Marievale, Transvaal, S Africa	113,826
Mineros de Antiguia, Columbia	46,819
Mineros del Choco, Columbia	14,294
Pamour Porcupine Mines Ltd, Canada	153,428
Noranda, Canada	220,050
President Brand, Orange Free State, S Africa	1,183,626
President Stern, Orange Free State, S Africa	914,615
Phelps Dodge, USA	46,432
Randfontein, Transvaal, S Africa	514,315
Real Del Monte y Pachuca, Mexico	18,447
Rosario Resources Corporation, Honduras	2,031
Rosario Dominican, SA	413,789
St Helena, Orange Free State, S Africa	841,179
Mineracao Morro Velho SA, Brazil	112,928
Sominki, Zaire	19,472
So African Land & Explor, Transvaal, S Africa	171,257

Gold production by company, 1976 (cont'd)

Company	*troy ounces*
Stilfontein, Transvaal, S Africa	528,188
Vaals Reefs, Transvaal, S Africa	2,122,090
Venterpost, Transvaal, S Africa	223,210
Virginia, Orange Free State, S Africa	–
Vlakfontein, Transvaal, S Africa	107,428
Welkom, Orange Free State, S Africa	431,846
Western Deep Levels, S Africa	1,431,734
Western Holdings, Orange Free State, S Africa	1,204,164
Western Areas, S Africa	734,452
Western Driefontein, Transvaal, S Africa	1,792,532
West Rand Consolidated, Transvaal, S Africa	–

Source: American Bureau of Metal Statistics Inc

Gold consumption, 1977 (excluding USSR)

Country	*metric tons*
Italy	220.0
Germany	88.0
Spain	54.0
UK and Ireland	45.4
France	37.4
Switzerland	32.5
Austria	12.6
Greece	10.0
Belgium	8.8
Yugoslavia	8.0
Netherlands	5.1
Sweden	3.4
Denmark	2.2
Finland	1.5
Cyprus and Malta	1.2
Norway	1.0
Portugal	0.1
Hungary	–
Total Europe	531.20
USA	162.3
Canada	22.0
Total North America	184.3
Brazil	20.0
Mexico	13.4
Venezuela	2.1
Columbia	2.0
Peru	0.9
Chile	0.7
Argentina	-8.0
Central America and Caribbean / Other Latin America	4.9
Total Latin America	36.0
Turkey	91.0
Iran	72.0
Arabia Yemen	45.5
Kuwait	22.5
Arabian Gulf States	13.2
Iraq, Syria, Jordan	24.0
Egypt	20.0
Israel	7.0
Lebanon	2.5
Total Middle East	297.7
India	40.5
Pakistan and Afghanistan	15.0
Sri Lanka	1.5
Bangladesh and Nepal	1.0
Total Indian Sub-Continent	58.0
Indonesia	30.0
Thailand	10.0

Gold consumption, 1977 (excluding USSR) cont'd

Country	*metric tons*
Singapore	8.8
Hong Kong	8.0
Taiwan	6.2
Malaysia	6.0
South Korea	5.2
Philippines	2.8
China	1.0
South Vietnam	—
Burma, Laos and Cambodia	- 0.5
Total excluding Japan	77.5
Japan	74.2
Total Far East	151.7
South Africa	92.8
Morocco/Algeria	20.0
Other Africa	5.0
Libyan	4.5
Tunisia	1.5
Total Africa	123.8
Australia	4.2
TOTAL	1386.9

Source: Consolidated Goldfields

Gold prices: annual average, 1945-1978 (London fixing)

Year	*US$/oz**	Year	*US$/oz**	Year	*US$/oz**
1945	34.34	1957	35.02	1969	41.09
1946	34.71	1958	35.10	1970	35.94
1947	34.71	1959	35.10	1971	40.80
1948	34.71	1960	35.62	1972	58.16
1949	36.36	1961	35.16	1973	97.32
1950	34.72	1962	35.07	1974	159.26
1951	34.72	1963	35.08	1975	161.02
1952	34.71	1964	35.12	1976	124.84
1953	34.71	1965	35.13	1977	147.98
1954	35.04	1966	35.19	1978	194.21
1955	34.98	1967	35.19		
1956	34.92	1968	38.56		

**troy ounce*

Price at 23 April 1979 $236.75 per troy ounce

Source: Minerais et Metaux, Consolidated Goldfields and Metal Bulletin

Silver ore: world production, 1976

Country	*troy ounces*
Argentina	2,379,155
Australia	25,096,869
Bolivia	5,092,677
Burma	739,467
Canada	40,886,099
Chile	7,285,358
China	1,286,030
Czechoslovakia	1,286,030
Finland	774,833
France	2,665,296
Germany East	1,028,824
Germany West	1,607,537
Greece	1,826,162
Honduras	3,182,923
Hungary	32,151
Ireland	842,349
Italy	1,559,311
Japan	9,304,425
Korea North	1,839,022
Korea South	1,607,537
Mexico	42,638,314
Morocco	2,729,598
Namibia (SW Africa)	1,099,555
Peru	38,130,780
Philippines	1,482,149
Poland	8,037,685
Portugal	337,583
Romania	1,286,030
South Africa	2,819,620
Spain	3,221,504
Sweden	4,700,438
USA	34,256,616
USSR	48,226,113
Yugoslavia	4,629,707
Zaire	2,472,392
TOTAL	313,083,926

Silver production by company, 1976

United States	*troy ounces*
The Anaconda Co (own mines)	3,204,061
Asarco Incorporated (own mines)	5,458,127
The Bunker Hill Company	
Bunker Hill Mine	1,185,174
Crescent Mine	371,168
Star Mine	548,083
Day Mines	1,053,865
Galena Mine	3,420,853
Hecla Mining Company	
Lakeshore Mine	41,054
Lucky Friday Mine	2,641,914
Mayflower Mine	–
Star Mine	238,028
Sunshine Mine	312,692

Silver production by company, 1976 cont'd

United States (cont'd)	*troy ounces*
Kennecott Copper Corporation	3,011,982
Magma Copper Company	
San Manuel Company	427,491
Superior Division	622,309
Phelps Dodge Corporation	2,158,996
St Joe Minerals Corporation	352,196
Sunshine	784,969
United Park City Mines	587,638
Mexico	
Industrial Minera Mexico, SA (only Monteorey Refinery)	17,210,621
Compania Minera de Cananea, SA	460,365
Cia Fresnillo, SA	4,807,456
Minera Frisco, SA	2,794,861
Compania de Real del Monte y Pachuca	3,508,635
Negociacion Minera Santa Maria de la Paz y Anekas, SA	1,058,438
Minas De San Luis, SA	1,902,015
Canada	
Anaconda American Brass Ltd – Britannia Operations	–
Cyprus Anvil Mining Corporation	639,000
Cominco Ltd	9,430,000
Consolidated Rambler Mines Ltd	95,700
Cupra Mines Ltd	48,219
D'Estrie Mining Co Ltd	160,286
Texasgulf Canada Ltd Div, Texasgulf Inc	8,501,217
Geco Division of Noranda Mines Ltd	1,570,000
Hudson Bay Mining and Smelting Co Ltd	1,220,853
Inco Ltd, Canada	1,560,882
Manitou Barvue	N/A
Pamour Porcupine Mines Ltd	69,817
Nigadou River Mines Ltd	576,143
Noranda Mines Ltd	17,140,980
Normetal	–
United Keno Hill	2,369,770
Weedon Mines Ltd	–
Other countries	
Aguilar, Argentina	1,749,952
Australian Mining & Smelting Ltd	3,885,096
Benquet Consolidated, Inc, Philippines	149,515
Bolidens, Sweden	6,362,535
BH South Limited, Australia	218,844
Centomin, Peru	19,227,700
Codelco, Chile	
Division Andina	391,113
Division Chuquicamata	4,422,466
Division Salvador	320,704
Division El Teniente	411,289
Empresa Minera Quechisla, Bolivia	2,599,227
Generale Des Carrieres Et Des Mines, Zaire	1,943,802
Gortdrum Mines (Ireland) Ltd	–
Huaron, Peru	2,134,972
Irish Base Metals Ltd	N/A
Mount Isa, Australia	14,183,796

Silver production by company, 1976 cont'd

Other countries (cont'd)	*troy ounces*
No 1 Mining Corp, Burma (refined only)	211,000
New Broken Hill Consolidated Ltd, Australia	(Reported under Australian Mining & Smelting Ltd)
Outokumpu Oy, Finland	773,257
Rosario Resources Corporation, Honduras	2,795,469
North Broken Hill Ltd, Australia	3,053,258
Penarroya and Affiliates	5,982,864
of which: Brazil	431,656
France	3,540,598
Greece	–
Italy	234,797
Spain	1,775,813
Tunisia	N/A
Prenssay – Boliden-Blei, GmbH, West Germany	3,147,620
Berzelins Metall Hutten GmbH, West Germany	N/A
Salsique, France	136,608
Compania Minerales Santader Inc, Peru	406,120
Tsumeb, Namibia (SW Africa)	1,174,000
Vielle Montagne, France	–
Zinc Corporation, Australia	(Reported under Australian Mining & Smelting Ltd)

Source: American Bureau of Metal Statistics Inc

Silver prices: annual average, 1945-1978

Year	US$/oz*	Year	US$/oz*	Year	US$/oz*
1945	0.52	1957	0.908	1969	1.79
1946	0.80	1958	0.89	1970	1.77
1947	0.72	1959	0.91	1971	1.55
1948	0.74	1960	0.91	1972	1.68
1949	0.72	1961	0.92	1973	2.56
1950	0.74	1962	1.08	1974	4.71
1951	0.89	1963	1.28	1975	4.42
1952	0.84	1964	1.29	1976	4.35
1953	0.85	1965	1.29	1977	4.61
1954	0.85	1966	1.29	1978	5.39
1955	0.89	1967	1.55		
1956	0.908	1968	2.14		

*troy ounce

Price at 25 April 1979 $7.49 per troy ounce

Source: J Aron – American Bureau of Metal Statistics, Metal Bulletin, Metals Week and Handy and Harman

Platinum: world production, 1976

Country	*troy ounces*
Canada	186,613
Columbia*	22,000
Japan	8,681
S Africa	1,938,348
USA	5,305
USSR	840,000
Total	3,000,947

Reserves 209 million oz.

**Crude platinum*

Platinum, major producers

Inco Ltd, Canada
Impala Platinum Ltd, S Africa
Lonrho Ltd, South Africa
Rustenburg Platinum Holdings Ltd, S Africa
Rustenburg Platinum Mines Ltd, S Africa
Texasgulf Inc, USA
Union Corp Ltd, S Africa
Western Platinum Ltd, S Africa
and the USSR

Source: Mining International Yearbook 1979, Financial Times

Platinum prices: annual average, 1945-1978 (New York)

Year	*US$/oz**	Year	*US$/oz**	Year	*US$/oz**
1945	35.00	1957	89.451	1969	121.667
1946	57.20	1958	64.925	1970	130.00
1947	59.09	1959	73.25	1971	120.524
1948	86.25	1960	81.729	1972	120.779
1949	73.36	1961	82.00	1973	150.036
1950	76.56	1962	82.00	1874	180.848
1951	90.00	1963	79.755	1975	164.005
1952	90.00	1964	87.985	1976	161.729
1953	91.238	1965	97.583	1977	162.00
1954	83.897	1966	99.167	1978	300.00
1955	85.978	1967	108.509		
1956	103.896	1968	114.50		

**troy ounce*

Price at 20 April 1979 $393.50 per troy ounce

Source: Metal Bulletin, Metals Week, Minerais et Metaux

Palladium: world production, 1975 and 1976

Country	*troy ounces*
Canada	184,463 (1976)
Columbia	N/A
Japan	13,981 (1975)
S Africa	683,322 (1976)
USA	10,963 (1975)
USSR	1,680,000 (1976)
Total	2,572,729
Reserves	177 million troy ounces

Source: Metal Bulletin

Palladium consumption, 1974

Country	*thousand troy ounces*
USA	960
Japan	800
Others	650
Total	2410

Source: US Bureau of Mines

Palladium prices: annual average, 1968-1978 (producer price)

Year	*US$/oz**	**Year**	*US$/oz**	**Year**	*US$/oz**
1968	45	1972	42	1976	51
1969	42	1973	78	1977	60
1970	38	1974	133	1978	80
1971	37	1975	93		

**troy ounce*

Source: Metal Bulletin

Rhodium: world production, 1975

Country	*troy ounces*
Canada	11,976
S Africa	63,199
USA	32
USSR	78,400
Total	153,607
Reserves	5.28 million ounces

Source: US Bureau of Mines

Rhodium prices: annual average, 1968-1978 (producer price)

Year	US$/oz*	Year	US$/oz*	Year	US$/oz*
1968	247	1972	197	1976	384
1969	240	1973	222	1977	441
1970	215	1974	329	1978	650
1971	200	1975	338		

** troy ounce*

Price at 20 April 1979 $700 per troy ounce

Source: Metal Bulletin

Iridium: world production, 1975

Country	*troy ounces*
Canada	8,782
S Africa	20,436
USA	225
USSR	53,000
Total	82,443
Reserves	5.91 million ounces

Source: US Bureau of Mines

Iridium prices: annual average, 1968-1978 (producer price)

Year	US$/oz*	Year	US$/oz*	Year	US$/oz*
1968	188	1972	162	1976	325
1969	185	1973	223	1977	298
1970	156	1974	391	1978	250
1971	152	1975	477		

** troy ounce*

Osmium: world production, 1975

Country	*troy ounces*
S Africa	262
USA	32
Total	294
Reserves	20,000 ounces

Source: US Bureau of Mines

Osmium prices: annual average, 1968-1978 (producer price)

Year	US$/oz*	Year	US$/oz*	Year	US$/oz*
1968	400	1972	212	1976	200
1969	335	1973	200	1977	175
1970	215	1974	200	1978	150
1971	210	1975	200		

* *troy ounce*

Price at 20 April 1979 $120-150 per troy ounce

Source: Metal Bulletin

Ruthenium: world production, 1975

Country	*troy ounces*
Canada	33,933
South Africa	13,112
USSR	159,000
Total	206,045
Approx Reserves	14.36 million ounces

Source: US Bureau of Mines

Ruthenium prices: annual average, 1968-1978 (producer price)

Year	US$/oz*	Year	US$/oz*	Year	US$/oz*
1968	58	1972	52	1976	60
1969	58	1973	52	1977	60
1970	56	1974	59	1978	45
1971	53	1975	60		

**troy ounce*

Price at 20 April 1979 $45 per troy ounce

Source: Metal Bulletin

Inflation Index: Index of the internal purchasing power of the pound sterling (1963 = 100)

1946	183.5	1958	110.6	1970	74.2
1947	171.8	1959	109.9	1971	67.8
1948	159.5	1960	108.8	1972	63.3
1949	155.8	1961	105.7	1973	57.5
1950	151.5	1962	101.8	1974	50.0
1951	138.9	1963	100.0	1975	40.0
1952	131.1	1964	96.8	1976	34.5
1953	128.9	1965	92.6	1977	30.0
1954	126.6	1966	89.2		
1955	122.4	1967	87.0		
1956	117.2	1968	83.2		
1957	113.6	1969	78.9		

Source: Metal Bulletin prepared by UK Central Statistical Office

Appendix 2:
Silver brands deliverable on the London Metal Exchange

Official list issued by the Committee of the London Metal Exchange of brands of silver deliverable in fulfilment of contracts for silver.

Silver deliverable against the Fine Silver Contract shall be in the form of bars in the weight range 450 to 1250 troy ounces.

Argentina:	Stella
Australia:	B.H.A.S. E.S.A. Erands
Belgium:	Société Générale Métallurgique de Hoboken SA Hoboken 999.7+ Hoboken 999+
Bulgaria:	M
Burma:	Burma Mines
Canada:	C.C.R. O.R.C. Tadanac
France:	Comptoir Lyon M.B.L.G. Compagnie des Métaux Précieux
Germany (East):	Mansfeld Heraeus
Germany (West):	Degussa Norddeutsche Affinerie
Holland:	Smelting Schones H.D.Z.
Italy:	M.P.
Japan:	Three Diamond Dowa NSS HM

Mexico:	Asarco-Monterey
	Cia Minera de Penoles SA
	Cia Metalurgica Penoles SA
	IMM – Monterrey
	Metalurgica Mexicana Penoles SA
	R. del M.
	S.A.M.
Peru:	C de P
	C. P. Peru
Poland:	Z.T.M.
South Africa:	R.R.Ld.
South West Africa:*	TCL
Spain:	Peñarroya
	Socemp
	Orispania
Sweden:	Boliden Silver (999)
Switzerland:	MP Métaux Précieux SA
United Kingdom:	B.L.Co
	Engelhard London
	J.M.
	J.M.C.
	J.M.C.F.
	Johnson Matthey London 999
	J.S.C.F.
	J.S.W.
	R
	S.S.Co
US	Asarco-Baltimore
	Asarco-Perth Amboy
	Asarco-Selby
	AS & R Co-Baltimore
	AS & R Co-Perth Amboy
	Selby Gold & Silver Refinery
	San Francisco, Cal
	Balbach
	B.E.R.
	Bunker Hill
	D.R.W.
	E
	Fisarco Amarillo Texas
	I.S.R.
	K.U.E.

*Namibia

US (cont.)	Raritan Seal of the US S-M – *(Warrants issued on and after 15/10/78 not good delivery)* U.M.S. Co U.S.S. Co
USSR	C.C.C.P.
Yugoslavia:	B.O.R. Trepca

Appendix 3:
Platinum: acceptable brands London/Zurich markets as at June 1979

London market

Impala
USSR
Engelhard
Johnson Matthey
Degussa
Comptoir Lyon – Alemand
Louyosta
Paris
INCO

Zurich market

SBC Paris
SBC Neuchatel
UBS Agores
Credit Valcambi

Appendix 4:
Silver contracts

The COMEX silver futures contract

The silver futures contract calls for the delivery of refined silver in standard bars during one of the specified future months at a price established through a reported official transaction made on the floor of COMEX.

Trading unit and grade: The contract calls for delivery of 5,000 troy ounces (6 per cent more or less) of refined silver bars of about 1,000 or 1,100 ounces each. The silver must be at least 999 fine (99.9 per cent) and must bear a brand approved and listed by COMEX.

Trading months: Trading in silver futures is conducted for delivery during the current calendar month, the immediately following two calendar months, as well as January, March, May, July, September, and December, during a seventeen-month period.

The reason silver futures trading is not conducted in each calendar month is to insure adequate liquidity. This limitation prevents diluting of trading over too many months and, thus, prevents price distortions based on relatively limited activity in any given month. However, silver is an expensive commodity, and for this reason the first three successive months are always traded so as to permit delivery at any time for those wishing to avoid storage and interest costs for nearby available material.

However, this limitation of delivery months does not undermine trading flexibility. If, for example, one wishes to sell silver in January for June delivery, which during January is not a trading month, one can sell an equal number of May and July contracts, thus obtaining, in effect, a June average. Your broker will explain to you that, for the purpose of hedging, the selling of July contracts can also be an effective hedge for a physical transaction. Furthermore, in April, June will become a delivery month, and a switch can then be made to allow June delivery.

Delivery: Deliveries of the silver against futures contracts on COMEX can be made at seller's option any time during any business day within the month specified in the contract. This silver must be made available at one of the warehouses licensed by COMEX. Licensed COMEX warehouses are all located in New York City, which is by far the largest centre of the US silver supply and demand.

Actually, the approved warehouses are bank vaults judged by COMEX to be safe and sufficiently well guarded to insure against theft. Periodic random examinations by independent surveyors are conducted in these vaults to ascertain the accuracy of the warrants as well as the chemical assay of the silver.

Price multiples: Price changes are registered in multiples of 1/10 of 1¢ per ounce. This minimum fluctuation is equivalent to $5 per contract. A fluctuation of 1¢ is, therefore, equivalent to $50 per contract.

Price fluctuation limitation: During any one market day, price fluctuations are limited to 20¢ per ounce above or below the settlement price for any traded months established at the close of the preceding business day. This limitation is made for the purpose of preventing dangerous fluctuations which may occur on unexpected news and to maintain a degree of stability in the market. However, this limitation does not apply to prices for the nearest, or delivery, month during the period in which this delivery may be made, since limitation in that month could interfere with actual deliveries.

The London Metal Exchange contract

Authorised 1st November, 1977

COPYRIGHT

SILVER CONTRACT FORM

Approved by the Board of Directors and by the Committee of the London Metal Exchange

LONDON,...

M...

I/We have this day sold to/bought from you, according and subject to the Rules and Regulations of the London Metal Exchange.

....

....Troy ounces (five per cent. either more or less) of

FINE SILVER

Price ....pence per ounce Troy, net plus/minus % to us

....

The appropriate Import Duty (if any) ruling on the prompt date to be for Buyer's Account.

Prompt ....

The sum of £..................................... (hereinafter referred to as "the initial margin") representing 10% of the value of this contract shall at the expiration of 3 market days from the date hereof be paid by you to us and in order to secure the due fulfilment by you of your obligations under this contract and to the intent that the value of the margin in relation to the contract shall at all times during the currency of the contract be maintained by you shall from time to time pay to us additional sums (hereinafter called "further margins") representing in total the difference for the time being between the value of the contract at the date of entering into the same and the current market value (of the silver the subject of the contract) provided that such further margin shall become payable if and as soon as (but not until) the said difference for the time being, less any further margin previously paid, shall be equal to at least 50% of the initial margin, and further margin thus require shall be paid within 3 market days of the occurrence of the matter aforesaid. The initial margin and further margin shall be paid in cash or in

the form of such other immediately negotiable security of equivalent value or bank guarantee as we at our discretion may accept.

This contract is made between ourselves and yourselves as principals, we alone being liable to you for its performance. The percentage (if any) charged by us to you is to be regarded simply as part of the price and may be shared by us with agents introducing the business, whilst we reserve the right also to charge a percentage or commission to any person from or to whom we may have bought or sold to cover our liability hereunder.

In the event of your failing to meet your engagements arising out of this or any other outstanding contract or contracts between us which are subject to the Rules and Regulations of the London Metal Exchange whether by failing to provide on the due date documents to meet sales or money to take up documents (as the case may be) or otherwise howsoever or of your failing to supply the margin and where necessary the further margin or margins or in the event of your suspending payment or becoming bankrupt or committing any act of bankruptcy or (being a Company) in the event of your going into liquidation whether voluntary or otherwise we reserve the right to close this contract and any other said outstanding contract or contracts if as and when we in our sole discretion shall so decide by selling out or buying in against you (as the case may be) and any differences arising therefrom shall be payable forthwith notwithstanding that the prompt day or other day originally stipulated for settlement may not have arrived.

Any delay in our enforcing any of our rights under this contract shall not be deemed to constitute a waiver thereof.

Members of the London Metal Exchange

SPECIAL RULES FOR SILVER

1. **Quality.**—All Silver delivered under this contract must be of a minimum fineness of ·999 in the form of bars in the weight range 450 troy ounces to 1250 troy ounces.

All Silver delivered must be of brands as listed on the London Metal Exchange approved list of Silver brands. Each bar must be impressed with the refiners weight, the brand, serial number and the assay.

2. **Settlement.**—Contracts shall be settled on exact quantities of 10,000 troy ounces at the official Settlement price quoted by the Committee operative on the prompt date, Buyer and Seller paying or receiving, as the case may be, the difference, if any, between the Settlement price and the contract price.

3. **Delivery.**—The Silver shall be delivered on the prompt date in any vault/warehouse listed for this purpose with the Committee at listed delivery points in seller's option. (Names of such vaults/warehouses can be obtained from the London Metal Exchange Office.) Warrants tendered in fulfilment of contracts shall be invoiced at the Settlement Price mentioned in Rule 2 above in parcels each of 10,000 troy ounces or a multiple thereof (each 10,000 troy ounces to be treated as a separate contract). Warrants shall be for 10,000 troy ounces (five per cent. either more or less) and may consist of one of the officially listed brands; each parcel of 10,000 troy ounces shall lie at one vault/warehouse. Rent shall be allowed on the invoice.

4. **Weights.**—Warrant weights in all cases shall be accepted as between buyer and seller.

5. **Warrants.**—Each Warrant must state the refiners weight, the brand, serial number and the assay of each bar.

6. **Exchange Control Regulations.**—If Amsterdam, Rotterdam or Hamburg

warrants are delivered to a resident of the United Kingdom not participating in the Bank of England Metals Scheme for dealings in Silver in fulfilment of this contract, the seller must issue a C.M. form in accordance with the procedure currently in force under the Scheme. The Buyer must conform with the requirements expressed on those parts of the C.M. form which he receives from the Seller.

7. **Disputes.**—Any question concerning formation and any dispute under this contract shall be notified to the Secretary of the London Metal Exchange in writing by the seller or the buyer or both of them jointly. Such question or dispute if not settled by agreement shall be referred to arbitration in accordance with the Rules and Regulations of the London Metal Exchange. The decision in writing of the Appeal Committee from the Award of the Arbitrators shall be a condition precedent to a Notice of Motion to remit or set aside the Award of the Arbitrators and the decision of the Appeal Committee or to an action being brought. The Uniform Law concerning the formation of contracts for the International Sale of Goods and the Uniform Law regulating the International Sale of Goods shall not apply.

CONTRACT RULES

Rule A
Members of the London Metal Exchange, in their dealings with other Members, shall be responsible to and entitled to claim against one another, and one another only, for the fulfilment of every Contract for Metals.

Rule B
In these Rules the expression 'Members of the London Metal Exchange' includes Firms and Companies who, although not themselves Subscribers to the Exchange, are represented and deal thereon by and through 'Representative Subscribers' to the Exchange acting as the representatives or Agents of such Firms or Companies.

Rule C
If any Member of the Metal Exchange fails to meet his engagements to another Member, whether by failing to provide on the due date documents (i.e. Bills of Lading, Warrants or Delivery Orders according to the metals dealt in) to meet sales made or money to pay for metals bought, or by making default in fulfilling any other obligation arising out of dealings made subject to the Rules and Regulations of the London Metal Exchange, notice of the default shall be given at once in writing to the Committee of the Exchange and the Committee shall immediately fix and publish a settlement price or prices as at the date of such communication to them for all contracts which the defaulter may have open under these Rules, whether with Members or with parties who are not Members. All such contracts shall forthwith be closed and balanced, by selling to or buying from the defaulting Member such metals as he may have contracted to deliver or take, at the settlement prices fixed for this purpose by the Committee, and any difference arising whether from or to the party in default shall become payable forthwith notwithstanding that the prompt day or other day originally stipulated for the settlement of the transaction may not have arrived. In fixing settlement prices under this Rule the Committee may in their discretion take into consideration the extent and nature of the transactions which the defaulting Member has open and any other circumstance which they may consider should affect their decision. In any case where the Committee shall be of opinion that the default is not due to the insolvency of the defaulter the Committee shall by resolution negative the application of this rule. Any claim arising out of a default not due to insolvency shall be settled by arbitration in the usual manner. This rule shall apply to cases in

which at or after the decease of a Member the engagements entered into by him are not duly met.

Rule D
In any Contract made subject to the Rules and Regulations of the London Metal Exchange between a Member and a non-Member, in the event of the Non-Member failing to meet his engagement arising out of any such contract whether by failing to provide on the due date documents to meet sales or money to take up documents (as the case may be) or otherwise howsoever or of his failing to supply or maintain such margin (if any) for which the Member is entitled to call and has called, or in the event of the Non-Member's suspending payment or becoming bankrupt or committing any act of bankruptcy or (being a Company) in the event of its going into liquidation whether voluntary or otherwise, the Member shall have the rights to close all or any such Contracts outstanding between them by selling out or buying in against the Non-Member (as the case may be) and any differences arising therefrom shall be payable forthwith notwithstanding that the prompt day or other day originally stipulated for settlement may not have arrived.

Rule E
Payments for Warrants or other documents (when deliverable under the Contracts) unless otherwise stipulated on the contract, shall be made by cash in London by cheque on a London *clearing* bank, either mode in Seller's option. The documents shall be tendered in London against the cash or cheque, as the case may be, and not later than 2.30 p.m. on the prompt or settling day.

Rule F
Contracts wherein Buyer or Seller (as the case may be) has the option to uplift or to deliver, prior to the prompt or settlement date by giving previous notice of his intention, shall have the notice reckoned by market days; such notices, unless otherwise stipulated at time of purchase or sale, shall be as follows: On a Contract with the option to uplift or to deliver during one calendar month or less, one day's notice shall be given; on a Contract with the option beyond one and up to two calendar months two days' notice shall be given; and on a Contract with the option beyond two and up to three calendar months three days' notice shall be given previous to the date on which delivery is required, or will be made. In the case of Silver on a Contract with the option beyond three and up to four calendar months four days' notice shall be given; on a Contract with the option beyond four and up to five calendar months five days' notice shall be given; on a Contract with the option beyond five and up to six calendar months six days' notice shall be given; on a Contract with the option beyond six and up to seven calendar months seven days' notice shall be given previous to the date on which delivery is required, or will be made. Notice shall be given for the whole quantity stated in the contract and shall be tendered in writing and delivered at the office of the seller of the option not later than noon on the day of notice. Rent shall only be allowed to Buyer to actual day of settlement; and there shall not be any allowance of interest for a payment made prior to the prompt date.

Rule G
Prompt or settlement dates falling on Saturday, Sunday, or a Bank Holiday which days are not market days, shall be settled as follows. Prompts falling on Saturday shall be settled on the Friday previous; but should the preceding Friday be a Bank Holiday the prompt shall be extended to the Monday following; should both the Friday preceding and the Monday following be Bank Holidays, the prompt shall be settled on the Thursday previous. Prompts falling on Sunday should be extended to

the Monday following, but should that Monday be a Bank Holiday the prompt shall be extended to the Tuesday following; should both the following Monday and Tuesday be Bank Holidays, the prompt shall then be extended to the Wednesday following. Prompts falling on a Bank Holiday shall be extended to the day following; and if the Bank Holiday falls on Friday the prompts shall be extended to the Monday following; but should the Friday be Good Friday, prompts falling on that day shall be settled on the Thursday previous. If Christmas Day falls on Monday, prompts falling on that day shall be extended to the Wednesday following, but if Christmas Day falls on Tuesday, Wednesday, Thursday, or Friday, prompts falling on that day shall be settled on the day previous.

Rule H

The establishment, or attempted establishment of a 'corner', or participation directly or indirectly in either, being detrimental to the interest of the Exchange, the Committee shall, if in their opinion a 'corner' has been or is in the course of being established, have power to investigate the matter and to take whatever action it considers proper to restore equilibrium between supply and demand. Any member or members may be required to give such information as is in his or their possession relative to the matter under investigation.

Rule J (OPTIONS)

On the day on which notice is due, the holder of the option shall, except in cases to which Rule C applies, declare in writing before 12 o'clock noon whether he exercises or abandons the option, and if he fails to make such declaration the option shall be considered as abandoned. Options (subject to Rule F above) may be declared for less than the total optional quantity in quantities of 25 tonnes for Copper-Electrolytic Wirebars, H.C.F.R. Wirebars, Cathodes or Fire Refined, 5 tonnes for Standard Tin, High Grade Tin, 25 tonnes for Standard Lead, 25 tonnes for Standard Zinc and 10,000 ounces for Silver or multiples thereof, only one declaration against each contract being allowed. In cases to which Rule C applies the prices fixed by the Committee, at which outstanding contracts are to be closed, shall equally apply to all option contracts; and all options shall be automatically determined, and be deemed to have been either exercised or abandoned according as the prices may be in favour of or against the defaulter and whether the defaulter be the Seller or the Buyer of an option, and the option money shall be brought into account. In contracts with optional prompts, the price which shall be taken as the basis of settlement shall be the settlement price fixed by the Committee under Rule C for the prompt most favourable to the holder of the option.

Rule K (CLEARING)

All contracts made between Members of the London Metal Exchange who are entitled to deal in the Ring, either for Copper-Electrolytic Wirebars, H.C.F.R. Wirebars, Cathodes or Fire Refined, Standard Tin, High Grade Tin, Standard Lead, Standard Zinc or Silver, shall be settled through the Clearing, except when a Member insists on his right to receive cash instead of cheque from the Member to whom he has sold, in which case the Seller shall give notice to his Buyer before noon on the market day preceding the settling day, and such transactions shall then be exempted from settlement through the Clearing. The Rules governing the Clearing of all contracts shall be those in existence at the time fixed for the fulfilment of the contract. Copies of such rules may be obtained from the Secretary of the Exchange.

Rule L

In the case of strikes, lock-outs, or other unforeseen contingencies in London, or other authorised port or point of delivery, which prevent or delay the discharge and/or warehousing of Copper-Electrolytic Wirebars, H.C.F.R. Wirebars, Cathodes or Fire Refined, Standard Tin, High Grade Tin, Standard Lead, Standard Zinc and/or Silver the Seller may be allowed to postpone delivery if he can prove to the satisfaction of the Committee (of which proof the Committee shall be the sole judge) that he does not hold available metal in warehouse or vault with which to fulfil his contracts and that he has metal of the requisite quality which has arrived in London or any other authorised port or point of delivery at least ten days prior to the earliest prompt for which relief is asked, or has metal of the requisite quality in his works, but the delivery, discharge and/or warehousing of which is prevented or delayed as aforesaid. He must also deposit with the Secretary of the Exchange such sums as the Committee may require but not exceeding £5 per tonne in the case of Copper, Lead and Zinc, £10 per tonne in the case of Tin and £5 per thousand ounces in the case of Silver. No interest will be allowed on deposits, which will be returned after delivery of Warrants. Should his application be passed by the Committee, he shall deposit documents or other proof to the satisfaction of the Committee with the Secretary of the Exchange, who shall issue Certificates for Copper, Lead and Zinc in quantities of 25 tonnes, Certificates for Tin in quantities of 5 tonnes and Certificates for Silver in quantities of 10,000 ounces. The Seller shall deliver these Certificates to his Buyer. The Certificates will then constitute a good delivery on the Clearing within the period stated thereon and differences must be settled on the prompt day. The holder of a Certificate must present it to the firm named thereon not later than 2.30 p.m. on the day following that on which he receives notice in writing from his Seller that the Warrant for the actual Copper, Tin, Lead, Zinc or Silver is ready. He must take up the Warrant against payment at the settlement price fixed on the preceding market day, receiving or paying any difference between this and the price mentioned on the Certificate. In the event of the price on the Certificate being above or below the settlement price operative on the day of delivery, the receiver shall pay or be paid the amount of any difference. No other payments shall pass except against delivery of the actual Warrant. In case of any dispute, the Committee's ruling to be final. A fee of £5 to be paid by the Applicants for each Certificate issued.

ARBITRATION

Rule 1

All disputes arising out of or in relation to contracts subject to the Rules and Regulations of the London Metal Exchange shall be referred to arbitration as hereinafter provided. The Executive Secretary of the Committee of the London Metal Exchange (hereinafter referred to as 'the Secretary') shall be notified of such disputes in writing and the party first notifying the difference shall at the time of such notification deposit with the Metal Market & Exchange Co. Ltd., the sum of £100. All such disputes shall be referred to two arbitrators, one to be appointed by each party to the difference from the Arbitration Panel of the London Metal Exchange, such arbitrators having power to appoint a third arbitrator from the Panel and having all the powers conferred on arbitrators by the Arbitration Act 1950 or any statutory modifications thereof for the time being in force. The Secretary shall be notified in writing by each party of the appointment of the arbitrators. The arbitration and any Appeal made pursuant to Rule 8 of these Rules from the Award of the Arbitrators to the Committee shall take place at the London Metal Exchange (unless mutually agreed by the Arbitrators and the parties to the dispute that the venue should be elsewhere in England or Wales) and English procedure and law shall be applied thereto.

Rule 2
Persons eligible for appointment to the Arbitration Panel shall be members of the Exchange, their partners or co-directors (as the case may be) or members of their staff. Appointment to and removal from the Panel shall be made, at their sole discretion, by the Committee of the London Metal Exchange who will also be responsible for maintaining a panel of sufficient size.

Rule 3
In the event of either, party to the difference (a) failing to appoint an arbitrator, or (b) failing to give notice in writing or by cable of such appointment to reach the other party within 14 days after receiving written or cabled notice from such other party of the appointment of an arbitrator (any notice by either party being given to the other either by cable or by registered post addressed to the usual place of business of such other party), or (c) in the case of death, refusal to act, or incapacity of an arbitrator, then, upon written or cabled request of either party an arbitrator shall be appointed from the said Arbitration Panel by the Committee of the London Metal Exchange.

Rule 4
In case the two arbitrators appointed as aforesaid, whether originally or by way of substitution, shall not within three calendar months after the appointment of the arbitrator last appointed deliver their Award in writing, or choose a third arbitrator, then the said Committee on the written request of either party shall appoint a third arbitrator selected from the said Arbitration Panel to act with the two aforesaid arbitrators.

Rule 5
The Award in writing of the arbitrators or any two of them shall be made and delivered in triplicate to the Secretary within a period of three calendar months from the date of the acceptance of the appointment by the arbitrator last appointed.

Rule 6
Every Award made pursuant to any provision of this Rule shall be conclusive and binding on the parties to the arbitration, subject to appeal as hereinafter mentioned.

Rule 7
The procedure upon an arbitration shall be as follows:

(a) Within a period of 21 days after the appointment of the second of the two arbitrators so appointed, each party shall deliver to the arbitrators and to each other a statement of case in writing with the originals, or copies, or any documents referred to therein. All such documents to be in the English language or accompanied by certified translations into English.

(b) If either party shall make default in delivering such statements and documents (due consideration being given to time occupied by mails) the arbitrators shall proceed with the case on the statement before them, provided always that, in the sole discretion of the arbitrators, an extension of time may be allowed for the delivery of such statements and documents.

(c) The arbitrators shall appoint a day for a hearing within 28 days, or such further time as the arbitrators shall in their sole discretion allow, after the expiry of the 21 days in accordance with Rule 7*(a)*, and shall give due notice in writing thereof to the parties, who may, and if required by the

arbitrators shall, attend and shall submit to examination by the arbitrators and produce such books and documents as the arbitrators may require. Each party shall be entitled to produce verbal evidence before the arbitrators.

(d) Neither Counsel, nor Solicitor shall be briefed to appear for either party without the consent of the arbitrators.

(e) The arbitrators may engage legal or other assistance.

(f) The arbitrators may adjourn the hearing from time to time, giving due notice in writing to the parties of the resumed hearing, and the arbitrators may, if they think fit, proceed with such a resumed hearing in the absence of either party or of both parties.

(g) Where any change takes place in the constitution of the tribunal of arbitrators, either by substitution or otherwise, the new tribunal shall appoint a day for the hearing which shall be not later than 28 days, nor earlier than 7 days, after the change. Each party, if desiring to do so, may submit an Amended Statement of Case, with a copy to the other party, which must reach the new tribunal within seven days of its appointment.

(h) In the event of a third arbitrator being appointed, the provisions contained in Section 9 Sub-Section 1 of the Arbitration Act 1950 shall not apply to any reference.

(i) The cost of the arbitration shall be at the sole discretion of the arbitrators. The arbitrators shall fix the amount of their remuneration. The Award shall state separately the amount of such costs and remuneration and by whom they shall be paid and whether the whole or any part of the deposit referred to in Rule 1 of these Rules shall be returned to the party lodging the same or be forfeited. In the event of either or both parties having been granted permission by the arbitrators to be legally represented at the hearing, the arbitrators may take into consideration any legal costs which have been incurred.

(j) The Award shall be deposited with the Secretary who shall forthwith give notice of receipt thereof in writing to both parties, and a copy of such Award shall be delivered to both parties on payment by either party of the costs specified in the Award, which payment shall not affect any provision of the Award.

(k) In the event that after the deposit referred to in Ruled 1 of these Rules has been made the parties to the arbitration shall (i) settle their differences; (ii) fail to proceed as directed by the arbitrators under sub-clause *(c)* of this Rule; (iii) fail to take up the Award within 28 clear days of notification being given under sub-clause *(j)* of this Rule, such deposit shall be forfeited.

(l) At the time of issuing their Award, all statements and all documents lodged with the arbitrators shall be delivered by them to the Secretary, by whom they shall be retained until the expiration of the time for giving notice of appeal, as hereafter mentioned, after which the Secretary shall, unless there shall be such appeal, return them to the parties concerned.

Rule 8

Either party shall have the right to appeal against the Award to the Committee of the London Metal Exchange.

Rule 9

The method of appeal against the Award shall be as follows:

(a) The party making the appeal shall (i) within 21 days of the date of the Award give notice in writing of such appeal to the Secretary, and to the other party and shall at the same time state the grounds for appeal.
(ii) Deposit with the Secretary the sum of £200, and in addition the sum, if any, which shall be payable under the Award by the Appellant.

(b) Upon the receipt of such Notice of Appeal the Committee shall within 4 weeks nominate not less than five members (hereinafter called 'the Appeal Committee') to hear the Appeal. Members of the Appeal Committee shall be members of the Committee of the London Metal Exchange and/or members of the Board of the Metal Market & Exchange Co. Ltd.

(c) The procedure on appeal shall as far as possible be similar to that above provided for the original hearing, except that all statements and documents delivered to the Secretary under Rule 7*(l)* shall be laid before the Appeal Committee, who may, however, require such further statements or statements or other information or documents from either or both of the parties as the Appeal Committee may think necessary. The provision of Rule 7*(k)* shall apply in like manner to the deposit referred to in sub-paragraph *(a)*(ii) of this Rule as the deposit in connection with the original hearing.

(d) The decision in writing of the majority of the Appeal Committee (which latter shall not at any time number less than five) shall be final and binding on all parties, and the Appeal Committee shall also decide whether the whole or any part of the said deposit of £2000 shall be returned to the Appellant or be forfeited.

(e) The Appeal Committee shall have the same discretion regarding costs as is given to the arbitrators under Rule 7*(i)* and shall fix the amount of their remuneration and direct by whom it shall be paid.

(f) All statements and all documents lodged with the Appeal Committee shall together with the Award, be deposited by them with the Secretary by whom they shall be retained until the costs and fees specified in the Awards have been paid by either party. On payment, which shall not affect any provision of the Award, a copy of the Award shall be delivered to both parties and all documents returned to the parties concerned.

Appendix 5:

Members of Commodity Exchange Inc (COMEX), New York and the London Metal Exchange (LME)

New York: **Commodity Exchange Inc (COMEX) trading members, as at October 1978**

M Abrams
120 E Hartsdale Ave, Hartsdale, NY 10530

T Adachi, Adachi Gold Co Ltd
Gusrae, Green & Kaplan
67 Wall St, New York, NY 10005

I Afram, Afram Bros, Inc
900 S Water St, Milwaukee, WI 53204

T Alt, Ray E Friedman & Co
c/o Commodity Exchange, Inc
4 World Trade Center, New York, NY 10048

J Arkin
300 S Wacker Dr, Chicago, IL 60606

R Arias, Mintz, Marcus & Co
4 World Trade Center, 8th Floor, New York, NY 10048

R Aron, J Aron & Co, Inc
160 Water St, New York, NY 10038

M Ashby, Minemet, Inc
450 Park Ave, New York, NY 10022

M Ashraf, c/o Eastern Trade Corp
Sheikha Bldg, PO Box 1376, Deira, Dubai, United Arab Emirates

D F Auciello, Great American Trading Co
4 World Trade Center, 8th Floor, New York, NY 10048

V W Augello
674 Keil St, Elmont, NY 11003

J J Baer, Northern Investment, SA
PO Box 14-330, Madrid, Spain

H F Baerwald
International Minerals & Metals Corp
919 Third Ave, New York, NY 10022

M R Baldini, Baldini, Proffitt, Reilly & Co
61 Broadway, Rm 2526, New York, NY 10006

R Barba, Clayton Brokerage Co of St Louis
No 2 Gate Field Dr, Greenwich, CT 06830

M D Barrett
80 Pine St, New York, NY 10005

F W Baur, Harmon, Lichtenstein & Co
4 World Trade Center, Rm 7170, New York, NY 10048

H Becker-Fluegel, NRT Metals, Inc
576 Fifth Ave, New York, NY 10036

S Bell, Stanley B Bell & Co
4 World Trade Center, 8th Floor, New York, NY 10048

M Belmont
4 World Trade Center, 8th Floor, New York, NY 10048

W H Berger, Cargill Investor Services, Inc
2 Broadway, Room 2800, New York, NY 10004

K G Bergman, Amax Copper, Inc
200 Park Ave, New York, NY 10017

V Besso, Intsel Corp
825 3rd Ave, New York, NY 10022

L Bilello, Stanley B Bell & Co
4 World Trade Center, 8th Floor, New York, NY 10048

R G Bird
45 N Point Dr, Colts Neck, NJ 07722

G H Bischoff, Sharps, Pixley, Inc
100 Wall St, New York, NY 10005

L J Blankenship, Shearson Hayden Stone, Inc
4 World Trade Center, 8th Floor, New York, NY 10048

P B Bleecker, Scholtz & Co, Inc
110 Wall St, New York, NY 10005

R Bleichroeder, Samuel Montagu & Co Ltd
114 Old Broad St, London EC2 2HY, England

E J Blot
1472 S Ocean Blvd, Palm Beach, FL 33480

L J Blum, Eisen & Blum, Inc
141 W Jackson Blvd, Chicago, IL 60604

G Boglione, Boys, Investment & Trade Ltd
AV 15, App 112, Auzere, Sion, Switzerland

O Boonshoft
1330 Winters Bank Tower, Dayton, OH 45402

J P Branco, Floor Broker Associates
4 World Trade Center, 8th Floor, New York, NY 10048

J J Brandler, Lee B Stern & Co Ltd
4 World Trade Center, 8th Floor, New York, NY 10048

S J Briggs, Floor Broker Associates
4 World Trade Center, 8th Floor, New York, NY 10048

A Brodsky
4 World Trade Center, 8th Floor, New York, NY 10048

J Brodsky
612 Howard Pl, Apt B, Madison, WI 53703

E J Browdy
c/o Anglo American Warehouse, Inc,
40th St & Packers Ave, Chicago, IL 60609

V Buccellato, B & B Commodities
4 World Trade Center, New York, NY 10048

J C Buck, ASARCO, Inc
120 Broadway, New York, NY 10005

O Burchard, The Ore & Chemical Corp
605 Third Ave, New York, NY 10016

M Burke
Smith Barney, Harris Upham & Co, Inc
120 Broadway, New York, NY 10019

M A Buscemi
4 World Trade Center, 8th Floor, New York, NY 10048

D R Campbell, Amalgamet, Inc
733 Third Ave, New York, NY 10017

A Capinegro, Lincolnwood, Inc
141 W Jackson Blvd, Chicago, IL 60604

C R Caruana, Dean Witter Reynolds, Inc
130 Liberty St, New York, NY 10006

E C Cashman, Cashman & Co
141 W Jackson Blvd, Chicago, IL 60604

S Chilewich, New York Hide Trading Co
120 Wall St, New York, NY 10005

J D Coffin, Drexel Burnham Lambert, Inc
60 Broad St, New York, NY 10004

P A Cohen, Herzfeld & Stern
30 Broad St, New York, NY 10004

J R Collins, Collins Commodities, Inc
175 W Jackson Blvd, Chicago, IL 60604

J J Conheeney
Merrill Lynch, Pierce, Fenner & Smith, Inc
One Liberty Plaza, 165 Broadway, New York, NY 10006

F J Coppola
Merrill Lynch, Pierce, Fenner & Smith, Inc
One Liberty Plaza, 165 Broadway, New York, NY 10006

H J Coyne, J Aron & Co, Inc
160 Water St, 19th Floor, New York, NY 10038

M L Coyne, J Aron Commodities, Corp
160 Water St, 19th Floor, New York, NY 10038

N S Crystal
PO Box 738, Union City, NJ 07087

P H Dalton Jr, Interstate Securities Corp
221 South Tryon St, Charlotte, NC 28202

J R D'Anna, Shearson Hayden Stone, Inc
4 World Trade Center, New York, NY 10048

R P D'Arcy, Amax Copper, Inc
200 Park Ave, New York, NY 10017

C D E Davis, Lonconex Ltd
29 Mincing Lane, London EC3R 7EU, England

N L Deak, Perera Co, Inc
29 Broadway, New York, NY 10006

M Decker, Bear, Stearns & Co
55 Water St, New York, NY 10041

A Del Re
4 World Trade Center, 8th Floor, New York, NY 10048

R DeMartino, Commodity International Co
84 William St, New York, NY 10038

S DeMicoli, Cerro Sales Corp
250 Park Ave, New York, NY 10017

H G Demarest, Easton & Co
One State St Plaza, New York, NY 10004

M H Denberg
4 World Trade Center, 8th Floor, New York, NY 10048

R F DeVellis, Federbush & Sabin
4 World Trade Center, 8th Floor, New York, NY 10048

T L Diamond, T L Diamond & Co, Inc
30 Rockefeller Plaza, New York, NY 10020

R Digiacomo, Balfour MacLaine International
88 Pine St, 9th Floor, New York, NY 10005

C Diliberto, Macro International Group, Inc
115 Broadway, Suite 1616, New York, NY 10006

J Diliberto, Macro International Group, Inc
115 Broadway, Suite 1616, New York, NY 10006

T H Dittmer, Ray E Friedman & Co
222 S Riverside Plaza, Chicago, IL 60606

R D Donchian, Shearson Hayden Stone, Inc
Two Greenwich Plaza, Greenwich, CT 06830

J P Donnelly Jr, Balfour, MacLaine, Inc
88 Pine St, New York, NY 10005

G E Doty, Goldman, Sachs & Co
55 Broad St, New York, NY 10004

P G Drogoul, Minemet, Inc
450 Park Ave, New York, NY 10022

S S Duberstein, Redel Trading Co, Inc
140 Cedar St, New York, NY 10006

F A Dubie
4 World Trade Center, 8th Floor, New York, NY 10048

A Durant, Lord Aldenham,
R J Rouse & Co Ltd
23 Blomfield St, London EC2M 7NL, England

D R Dustin, Precious Metals Corp of America
5 World Trade Center, Suite 7229, New York, NY 10048

C Edelstein, J Aron Commodities, Corp
4 World Trade Center, New York, NY 10048

H G Eisenberg
Brandeis, Goldschmidt & Co, Inc
919 Third Ave, New York, NY 10022

I Ergas
1199 Park Ave, New York, NY 10028

J J Ezzo, Mintz, Marcus & Co
4 World Trade Center, 8th Floor, New York, NY 10048

P K Falkenrath, Intsel Commodities, Inc
825 Third Ave, New York, NY 10022

S Fashena, First Wall Street Settlement Corp
14 Wall St, New York, NY 10005

C Federbush, Federbush & Sabin
225 E 73rd St, New York, NY 10021

H D Ferer, Aaron D Ferer & Sons Co
909 Abbot Dr, Omaha, NE 68102

D A Ferretti, Insilco Corp
500 S Broad St, Meriden, CT 06450

S H Fields, First Wall Street Settlement Corp
14 Wall St, 8th Floor, New York, NY 10005

R J Fisher
4 World Trade Center, 8th Floor, New York, NY 10048

M P Fitzgerald, Balfour, MacLaine, Inc
785 Poole Ave, Hazlet, NJ 07730

T P Fletcher
14 Noel Lane, Muttontown, NY 11753

F J Forlenza Sr, Felix J Forlenza & Co
16 W Granada Dr, Bucktown, NJ 08723

F J Forlenza Jr, Felix J Forlenza & Co
4 World Trade Center, 8th Floor, New York, NY 10048

S Forlenza
4703 Park Jacaranda, Calabasas, CA 91302

E L Frank, Philipp Brothers Div of Engelhard Minerals & Chemical Corp
1221 Ave of the Americas, New York, NY 10020

A L Freeman, Rosenthal & Co
4 World Trade Center, New York, NY 10048

A Fried Jr, Albert Fried & Co
77 Water St, New York, NY 10005

K A Friedlander
Brandeis, Goldschmidt & Co, Inc
919 Third Ave, New York, NY 10022

M A Fromer, Lewis & Peat Trading, Inc
460 Park Ave, New York, NY 10022

G J Gange, UV Industries, Inc
437 Madison Ave, New York, NY 10022

G P Garbe
588 Rose Blvd, Baldwin, NY 11510

R L Gardner
4 World Trade Center, 8th Floor, New York, NY 10048

D J Garrison
90 Kingfisher Dr, Middletown, NJ 07748

R Geissler, Easton & Co
One State St Plaza, New York, NY 10004

A G Gero, Drexel Burnham Lambert, Inc
4 World Trade Center, 8th Floor, New York, NY 10048

J Gill
PO Box 159, 1012 Lausanne, Chailly, Switzerland

M L Ginzberg, Primary Industries Corp
666 Fifth Ave, New York, NY 10019

M Glassberg, Ag-Met, Inc
PO Box 523, Hazleton, PA 18201

W Glazier, Shearson Hayden Stone, Inc
80 Pine St, New York, NY 10005

B I Goldberg, J Aron Commodities Corp
4 World Trade Center, New York, NY 10048

H Goodman
7851 S Ashland Ave, Chicago, IL 60620

M J Goodman
54 Levering Circle, Bala Cynwyd, PA 19004

N I Gosberg, N I Gosberg & Co, Inc
One Horizon Rd, Apt 1020, Fort Lee,
NJ 07024

A P Graham, NMR Metals, Inc
One Rockefeller Plaza, New York, NY 10000

J S Granger, Granger & Co
111 Broadway, New York, NY 10006

L Gray, Gray International, Inc
1271 Ave of the Americas, New York,
NY 10020

M Greenberg
4 World Trade Center, 8th Floor, New York,
NY 10048

S Greenberg, Balfour, MacLaine, Inc
88 Pine St, New York, NY 10005

R G Gremald, Ametalco, Inc
530 Fifth Ave, New York, NY 10036

R S Griffin
141 W Jackson Blvd, Room 1580, Chicago,
IL 60604

W J Griffin, Harmon, Lichtenstein & Co
4 World Trade Center, New York, NY 10048

H Grillo, Wilhelm Grillo Handelsgesellshaft
AM Grillo Park 5, Duisborg Hamborn,
West Germany

M A Grisez, Billiton Metals & Ores USA, Inc
600 Fifth Ave, New York, NY 10020

E R Haboush, Galaxy Diamond Corp
48 W 48th St, New York, NY 10036

P H Halladin
85 Hillcrest Dr, Upper Saddle River,
NJ 07458

H A Handleman
4 World Trade Center, 8th Floor, New York,
NY 10048

J H Hanemann, Felix J Forlenza & Co
4 World Trade Center, 8th Floor, New York,
NY 10048

R B Harmon, Harmon, Lichtenstein & Co
4 World Trade Center, Room 7170,
New York, NY 10048

D Harris, Richardson Securities, Inc
40 Wall St, New York, NY 10005

H U Harris Jr
Smith Barney, Harris Upham & Co, Inc
1345 Ave of the Americas, New York,
NY 10020

J E Harris
150 E Palmetto Park Rd, Boca Raton,
FL 33432

C Hatten
ACLI International Commodity Services, Inc
110 Wall St, New York, NY 10005

S Haydak, Easton & Co
4 World Trade Center, 8th Floor, New York,
NY 10048

H J Heinold, Heinold Commodities, Inc
222 S Riverside Plaza, Chicago, IL 60606

R Helfer, Helfer Commodities Corp
5 World Trade Center, New York, NY 10048

R Hendricks, Hendricks & Co
4 World Trade Center, PO Box 324,
New York, NY 10048

P J Henwood, Continental Grain Co
277 Park Ave, New York, NY 10017

J J Herman, c/o New York Cotton Exchange
4 World Trade Center, 8th Floor, New York,
NY 10048

R J Herstein
4 World Trade Center, 8th Floor, New York,
NY 10048

A Hettena, Republic Clearing Corp
450 Fifth Ave, New York, NY 10018

L A Hockstader II
L F Rothschild, Unterberg, Towbin
55 Water St, New York, NY 10041

E W Hoffstatter Jr, Sharps, Pixley, Inc
100 Wall St, New York, NY 10005

J J Hohenberg, The Hohenberg Co
PO Box 193, Memphis, TN 38013

F F Horn, Bache Halsey Stuart Shields, Inc
100 Gold St, New York, NY 10038

A C Israel, ACLI International, Inc
110 Wall St, New York, NY 10005

R Jacobson, Reading Industries, Inc
789 Downing St, Teaneck, NJ 07666

G Jaffe, Mintz, Marcus & Co
4 World Trade Center, New York, NY 10048

H G Jarecki, Mocatta Metals Corp
4 World Trade Center, Suite 5200, New York,
NY 10048

R W Jarecki, Brody, White & Co, Inc
4 World Trade Center, Suite 5200, New York,
NY 10048

D M Jenkins, London, Polanish Jenkins, Inc
4 World Trade Center, 8th Floor, New York,
NY 10048

D T Johnston, E F Hutton & Co, Inc
One Battery Park Plaza, New York, NY 10004

J L Johnston III
Conti Commodity Services, Inc
4 World Trade Center, Suite 774, SE Plaza Bldg, New York, NY 10048

J W Johnston, Gold Fields American Corp
230 Park Ave, New York, NY 10017

D E Jones
4 World Trade Center, 8th Floor, New York, NY 10048

D Jones, Arrow Manufacturing Co
885 Freeway Drive North, Columbus, OH 43229

P P Jones, Floor Broker Associates
4 World Trade Center, 8th Floor, New York, NY 10048

E J Karmin, Mintz, Marcus & Co
4 World Trade Center, New York, NY 10048

E Katz, Adolph Hirsch & Co
500 Fifth Ave, Suite 17, New York, NY 10036

G Kaufman
4 World Trade Center, 8th Floor, New York, NY 10048

E J Kennedy, Dean Witter Reynolds, Inc
2 Broadway, New York, NY 10004

B Kessner
67 Navajo Ave, Lake Hiawatha, NJ 07034

H S Kipnis, H S Kipnis & Co
209 S LaSalle St, Chicago, IL 60604

M Klein, Klein & Co
170 Broadway, Room 806, New York, NY 10006

R Klein, Klein & Co
170 Broadway, Room 806, New York, NY 10006

A M Kohl, Woodland Investment Partners
1401 N Western Ave, Lake Forest, IL 60045

A Kraus
Continental Copper & Steel Industries, Inc
12 Commerce Dr, Cranford, NJ 07016

I Kreitner, Wark Trading Co
4 World Trade Center, New York, NY 10048

I W Kuhlik
4 World Trade Center, 8th Floor, New York, NY 10048

M D Kurzrok, Lehman Bros, Kuhn Loeb, Inc
55 Water St, New York, NY 10041

R G LaFroscia, Ferriso, LaFroscia & Co
4 World Trade Center, 8th Floor, New York, NY 10048

W T Lakin
4 World Trade Center, 8th Floor, New York, NY 10048

D M Lambert, E P Lambert Co
1416 First National Tower, Akron, OH 44308

A H Lamborn III
Shearson Hayden Stone, Inc
4 World Trade Center, 8th Floor, New York, NY 10048

W C Layton Jr
Mine Brook Rd, Far Hills, NJ 07931

M Lazarus
4 World Trade Center, 8th Floor, New York, NY 10048

L H Leathers, Shearson Hayden Stone, Inc
One Western Union International Plaza, New York, NY 10004

G J Leinsdorf, Philipp Brothers Div of Engelhard Minerals & Chemicals Corp
1221 Ave of the America, New York, NY 10020

N S Leist
c/o New York Mercantile Exchange
4 World Trade Center, New York, NY 10048

G L Lennard, Gerald Metals, Inc
One Battery Park Plaza, New York, NY 10004

R Levenson, Intramet Corp
437 Madison Ave, New York, NY 10022

M H Levine, Mark H Levine & Co
4 World Trade Center, 8th Floor, New York, NY 10048

L Levy, Oppenheimer & Co, Inc
One New York Plaza, New York, NY 10004

M Levy, Levy Commodities
222 S Riverside Plaza, Chicago, IL 60606

G M Levyns, Metal Traders, Inc
445 Park Ave, New York, NY 10022

E Leytess, Leytess Metal & Chemical Corp
500 Fifth Ave, New York, NY 10036

G Lichtenstein
4 World Trade Center, 8th Floor, New York, NY 10048

C Lichtman, J Lichtman & Sons
241 Freylinghuysen Ave, Newark, NJ 07114

M Liebman, M Lib/Ras International
222 S Riverside Plaza, Chicago, IL 60606

N Lion, Phillip & Lion
Moor House, London Wall, London
EC2Y 5AR, England

A Lipper III, Arthur Lipper Corp
176 Broadway, New York, NY 10038

F A Lisi
4 World Trade Center, 8th Floor, New York, NY 10048

N J Lisi
4 World Trade Center, 8th Floor, New York, NY 10048

F A Lissauer
Associated Metals & Minerals Corp
30 Rockefeller Plaza, New York, NY 10020

M W Lissner, Lissner Minerals & Metals, Inc
1000 N North Branch St, Chicago, IL 60622

D Little, General Cable Corp
500 W Putnam Ave, Greenwich, CT 06830

J L Loeb Jr
Loeb Rhoades Hornblower & Co
375 Park Ave, New York, NY 10022

R E Loewenberg
R E Loewenberg Capital Management Corp
450 Park Ave, New York, NY 10022

A O London
4 World Trade Center, 8th Floor, New York, NY 10048

A Lotterman, Delos Commodities, Inc
4 World Trade Center, New York, NY 10048

A G Lowenthal, Cowen & Co
One Battery Park Plaza, New York, NY 10004

E W MacLennan
C Tennant, Sons & Co of NY
PO Box 9300, Minneapolis, MN 55440

M L Maduff, Maduff & Sons, Inc
222 S Riverside Plaza, Chicago, IL 60606

W Malinchak
4 World Trade Center, 8th Floor, New York, NY 10048

C J Maneri
70 Fox Hunt Cres, Oyster Bay Cove,
PO Syosset, NY 11791

J Manne
839 Ashland Ave, River Forest, IL 60305

H R Marcus, Mintz, Marcus & Co
4 World Trade Center, 8th Floor, New York, NY 10048

M Marcus, Commodities Corp
Mount Lucas Rd, Princeton, NJ 08540

E Margulies, Lonray (Sugar), Inc
77 Water St, New York, NY 10005

S C Markoff, A-Mark Trading Corp
United California Bank Bldg, 9601 Wilshire Blvd, Suite 2, Beverly Hills, CA 90210

N Marone, E Modet & Co, Inc
24 Lundi Ct, Staten Island, NY 10314

M Marx, United Equities Commodities Co
160 Broadway, New York, NY 10038

G A Mattana
27 Partridge Dr, Roslyn, NY 11576

C Mattey, Bache Halsey Stuart Shields, Inc
100 Gold St, New York, NY 10038

R E McDonnell
Commodity International Co
84 William St, New York, NY 10038

J M McHale
4 World Trade Center, 8th Floor, New York, NY 10048

M Mehl
4 World Trade Center, 8th Floor, New York, NY 10048

S R Meierfeld, Ray E Friedman & Co
4 World Trade Center, New York, NY 10048

D W Merriman
151 E 80th St, New York, NY 10021

D W Mesker, A G Edwards & Sons, Inc
One North Jefferson, St Louis, MO 63103

C Miller
Paine, Webber, Jackson & Curtis, Inc
25 Broad St, New York, NY 10004

H Mintz
2200 Park Lane, Hollywood, FL 33021

L A Mintz, Mintz, Marcus & Co
4 World Trade Center, 8th Floor, New York, NY 10048

H Monahan, Dean Witter Reynolds, Inc
c/o Commodity Exchange, Inc
4 World Trade Center, New York, NY 10048

J E Moore, Harmon, Lichtenstein & Co
4 World Trade Center, Room 7170,
New York, NY 10048

J F Moore, Harmon, Lichtenstein & Co
4 World Trade Center, Room 7170,
New York, NY 10048

J E P Moore, J Aron & Co
160 Water St, New York, NY 10038

J L Morace
457 Ridge Rd, Mahwah, NJ 07430

O J Morrissey
500 E 77th St, Apt 2025, New York, NY 10021

R A Moskowitz, Ram Commodities, Inc
4 World Trade Center, New York, NY 10048

S B Mudd, Handy & Harman
850 Third Ave, New York, NY 10022

E Mugdan, OCC Commodity, Inc
605 Third Ave, New York, NY 10016

J M Murray, E F Hutton & Co, Inc
4 World Trade Center, 8th Floor, New York, NY 10048

E Nadler
126 E 61st St, New York, NY 10021

A Napoletano
4 World Trade Center, New York, NY 10048

N L Nathanson, N L Nathanson & Co
460 North St, Greenwich, CT 06830

M H Nelson
4 World Trade Center, 8th Floor, New York, NY 10048

R Nessim, Philipp Brothers Div of Engelhard Minerals & Chemical Corp
1221 Ave of the Americas, New York, NY 10020

H Neu, Hugo Neu & Sons, Inc
380 Madison Ave, Suite 1710, New York, NY 10017

E G Newman, Chilewich Sons & Co
120 Wall St, New York, NY 10005

J Nordlicht
4 World Trade Center, 8th Floor, New York, NY 10048

J A Novak
16-66 Bell Blvd, Bayside, NY 11360

T P O'Hare
Merrill Lynch, Pierce, Fenner & Smith, Inc
One Liberty Plaza, 165 Broadway, New York, NY 10006

E J Oliveri
4 World Trade Center, 8th Floor, New York, NY 10048

C Oliverio
4 World Trade Center, 8th Floor, New York, NY 10048

J M Ondo
4 World Trade Center, 8th Floor, New York, NY 10048

R Oppenheimer, Mel Schnell & Co
c/o Commodity Exchange, Inc
4 World Trade Center, New York, NY 10048

J Orefice, c/o Commodity Exchange, Inc
4 World Trade Center, New York, NY 10048

M Parsoff, Lee B Stern & Co Ltd
141 W Jackson Blvd, Chicago, IL 60604

R B Paruch, Floor Broker Associates
4 World Trade Center, New York, NY 10048

D E Peiser, Kawama Securities Corp
50 Broadway, Room 1801, New York, NY 10004

R N Peters, Peters & Co
141 W Jackson Blvd, Chicago, IL 60604

M Piazza, Mintz, Marcus & Co
4 World Trade Center, 8th Floor, New York, NY 10048

J J Place
Merrill Lynch, Pierce, Fenner & Smith, Inc
165 Broadway, One Liberty Plaza, New York, NY 10006

R C Podewils, C Tennant, Sons & Co of NY
PO Box 9300, Minneapolis, MN 55440

F Polanish, London, Polanish Jenkins, Inc
4 World Trade Center, New York, NY 10048

J R Poulat, Sociedad Financiera De Industria y Descuento, SA
Av Fco I, Madero No 42, PB, Mexico, DF, Mexico

M Powers
Thomson McKinnon Securities, Inc
One New York Plaza, New York, NY 10004

H A Pratt, Cerro Sales Corp
250 Park Ave, New York, NY 10017

B Pressner, Pressner Trading Corp
4 World Trade Center, 8th Floor, New York, NY 10048

G E Preston, SNW Commodities Ltd
Rayner House, 39 Hatton Garden, London EC1N 8BX, England

A G W Prockter
Billiton-Enthoven Metals Ltd
Colonial House, Mincing Lane, London EC3R 7DR, England

B Quint, Easton & Co
4 World Trade Center, 8th Floor, New York, NY 10048

L Rabinowitz, Bear, Stearns & Co
55 Water St, New York, NY 10041

A Racz, Philips, Appel & Walden, Inc
111 Broadway, New York, NY 10006

C E Rasher, McMahon Iron & Metal Co, Inc
3300 Conner St, Bronx, NY 10475

I Redel, Redel Trading Co, Inc
140 Cedar St, New York, NY 10006

O F Rehders
c/o New York Cotton Exchange
4 World Trade Center, 8th Floor, New York, NY 10048

E Reynolds, Spiral Metal Co, Inc
515 Madison Ave, New York, NY 10022

M Rich, Marc Rich & Co, Inc
280 Park Ave, New York, NY 10017

A J Ritholtz
c/o New York Cotton Exchange
4 World Trade Center, 8th Floor, New York, NY 10048

A A Rosa, Rosa Commodities
4 World Trade Center, New York, NY 10048

S Rosenberg
425 E 58th St, New York, NY 10022

F Rosenblatt, Primary Metal & Mineral Corp
666 Fifth Ave, New York, NY 10019

S Rothberg
N 1406 Park Towne Pl, Philadelphia, PA

R E Rowland Jr
4 World Trade Center, 8th Floor, New York, NY 10048

D S Rubin
Thomson McKinnon Securities, Inc
One New York Plaza, New York, NY 10004

A J Rudner, Felix J Forlenza & Co
4 World Trade Center, 8th Floor, New York, NY 10048

H Sacks, Brandeis, Goldschmidt & Co (Commodities), Inc
919 Third Ave, New York, NY 10022

R Saitta, Bache Halsey Stuart Shields, Inc
100 Gold St, New York, NY 10038

J A Samuel, J A Samuel & Co
233 Broadway, New York, NY 10007

J N Santagata, Mintz, Marcus & Co
4 World Trade Center, 8th Floor, New York, NY 10048

E Santamaria, E Santamaria & Co, Inc
PO Box 2015, Manila, Philippines

P Sarpi, c/o New York Cocoa Exchange, Inc
30 Fulton St, New York, NY 10038

A H Schmidt-Fellner, Amax, Inc
2 Greenwich Plaza, Greenwich, CT 06830

A Schneiderman
180 Lakeside Drive S, Lawrence, NY 11559

M Schnell, Mel Schnell Co
4 World Trade Center, 8th Floor, New York, NY 10048

F G Schreiber, Lambros Metals, Inc
500 Fifth Ave, New York, NY 10036

M L Schultz, ACLI Metal & Ore Co
110 Wall St, New York, NY 10005

H Schwartz
140 Poplar Dr, Roslyn, NY 11576

M Sepenuk
21 Hyatt Ave, Newark, NJ 07105

N N Shak
22 Riverside Dr, Apt A-2, Cranford, NJ 07016

I E Shein, ACLI International, Inc
110 Wall St, New York, NY 10005

M Sherman, RMI Metals, Inc
One Main St, Mapleville, RI 02839

R Sicuranza
4 World Trade Center, 8th Floor, New York, NY 10048

T J Silk
4 World Trade Center, 8th Floor, New York, NY 10048

A P Silverberg
4 World Trade Center, 8th Floor, New York, NY 10048

B Sirota, General Trading Co, Inc
300 71st St, Room 440, Miami Beach, FL 33141

N L Sirota
115 Broadway, Room 1818, New York, NY 10006

E G Smith, Albert Trostel & Sons Co
800 N Marshall St, Milwaukee, WI 53202

J J Smith, Fahnestock & Co
110 Wall St, New York, NY 10005

A S Snyder, Trans World Metals, Inc
770 Lexington Ave, New York, NY 10022

I Solomon, ACLI International Commodity Services Corp
110 Wall St, New York, NY 10005

J M Soriano, Ansor Corp
1351 Washington Blvd, Stamford, CT 06902

A C Speyer Jr
1202 Benedum Trees Bldg, Pittsburgh, PA 15222

P Speziale Jr, Heinold Commodities, Inc
15 Maiden St, New York, NY 10038

J S Spiller, Mintz, Marcus & Co
4 World Trade Center, 8th Floor, New York, NY 10048

L W Steib
1647 Burnett St, Brooklyn, NY 11229

E A Stein
4 World Trade Center, 8th Floor, New York, NY 10048

R R Stemland
Paine, Webber, Jackson & Curtis, Inc
25 Broad St, 19th Floor, New York, NY 10004

A Steo, Shearson Hayden Stone, Inc
4 World Trade Center, 8th Floor, New York, NY 10048

J Stern, Stern & Stern Securities, Inc
110 Wall St, New York, NY 10005

L B Stern, Lee B Stern & Co Ltd
141 W Jackson Blvd, Chicago, IL 60604

J F Stewart
Loeb Rhoades Hornblower & Co
72 W Adams St, Chicago, IL 60603

D A Suskind, J Aron & Co, Inc
160 Water St, 19th Floor, New York, NY 10038

S Tanne
251 Central Park W, New York, NY 10024

C P Tant, Truebner & Co, Inc
130 John St, New York, NY 10038

R A H Tejani, Trans World Agencies
PO Box 648, Dubai, United Arab Emirates

C Terrein, Financiera Banamex, SA
Isabel La Catolica No 39, Mexico, 1, DF

E F Thaute, E F Hutton & Co, Inc
One Battery Park Plaza, New York, NY 10004

T Thomte, Thomte & Co, Inc
47 Commercial Wharf, Boston, MA 02110

J D Tuck, Drexel Burnham Lambert, Inc
80 Broad St, New York, NY 10004

P N Tuomey
4 World Trade Center, 8th Floor, New York, NY 10048

D C Turman
4 World Trade Center, 8th Floor, New York, NY 10048

P D F Varral, Johnson Matthey Bankers Ltd
5 Lloyds Ave, London EC3N 3DB, England

J Voe, Ray E Friedman & Co
c/o Commodities Exchange Center, Inc
PO Box 378, New York, NY 10048

J Vuillequez, Metal Traders, Inc
60 East End Ave, New York, NY 10028

J A Wade Jr
One Beekman Pl, New York, NY 10022

J Wagner
1957 Kimball St, Brooklyn, NY 11234

M R Wagner
1957 Kimball St, Brooklyn, NY 11234

H A Wall, Harvey Wall Co
600 Ave Conde 'F', Coral Gables, FL 33134

L S Walsh
4 World Trade Center, 8th Floor, New York, NY 10048

R Walton
4 World Trade Center, 8th Floor, New York, NY 10048

N D Waltuch
Conti Commodity Services, Inc
4 World Trade Center, Suite 774, SE Plaza Bldg, New York, NY 10048

A Weeks, Macro International Group, Inc
4 World Trade Center, 8th Floor, New York, NY 10048

L H Weiss
15 Percheron Lane, Roslyn Heights, NY 11577

H J Weissblatt, Brody, White & Co, Inc
4 World Trade Center, Suite 5200, New York, NY 10048

P Weissman
Liberty Smelting Works (1962) Ltd
PO Box 840, Postal Station A, Montreal, Quebec, Canada H3C 2V5

H C Weltzein Jr
209 Bear Ridge Rd, Pleasantville, NY 10570

G J Westheimer
4 World Trade Center, 8th Floor, New York, NY 10048

S Westheimer
6080 Northwest 44th St, Lauderhill, FL 33313

P I Willensky
Loeb Rhoades Hornblower & Co
42 Wall St, New York, NY 10005

R Willstatter
Gerald Commodity Services, Inc
One Battery Park Plaza, New York, NY 10004

R Winzap
Bullion Exchange & Trading Co Ltd
PO Box 2353, CH 1002 Lausanne,
4 Ave De La Gare, CH 1003 Lausanne, Switzerland

I Witkin
82 Wall St, New York, NY 10005

W I Witkin
113 Campfire Rd, Chappaqua, NY 10514

F F Wolff, Rudolf Wolff & Co Ltd
Knollys House, 11 Byward St,
London EC3R 5ED, England

G E Woodburn
Precious Metals Corp of America
5 World Trade Center, Suite 7229, New York, NY 10023

E J Young Jr
Clayton Brokerage Co of St Louis, Inc
1341 Andrew Dr, Glendale, MO 63105

B C Zins
4 World Trade Center, 8th Floor, New York, NY 10048

The London Metal Exchange, member companies, as at January 1979. A star indicates ring dealing members.

Amalgamated Metal Corp Ltd
Adelaide House, London Bridge, London EC4R 9DT
Tel: 01-626 4521, Telex: 888701,
Cables: Amalgameco London

Amalgamated Metal Trading Ltd*
2 Metal Exchange Bldgs, Leadenhall Ave,
London EC3V 1LD
Tel: 01-626 4521, Telex: 888704

Ambores Ltd
27 Marylebone Rd, London NW1 5JS
Tel: 01-486 4642

Ametalco Ltd
29 Gresham St, London EC2V 7DA
Tel: 01-606 8800, Telex: 885541,
Cables: Nucliform London EC2

Ametalco Merchanting Ltd
1 Noble St, London EC2V 7DA
Tel: 01-606 8800, Telex: 885541

Ametalco Trading Ltd*
29 Gresham St, London EC2V 7DA
Tel: 01-606 8800, Telex: 885541,
Cables: Nucliform London EC2

AM & S Europe Ltd
PO Box 237, 1 Redcliff St, Bristol BS99 7EA
Tel: 0272-290421, Telex: 449502

Anglo Chemical Metals Ltd*
Gillett House, 55 Basinghall St, London EC2V 5HN
Tel: 01-606 0811, Telex: 886767

Anglo Chemical & Ore Ltd
Gillett House, 55 Basinghall St, London EC2V 5HN
Tel: 01-606 0811, Telex: 885168

Anmercosa Sales Ltd
40 Holborn Viaduct, London EC1P 1AJ
Tel: 01-353 1545, Telex: 264791

Morris Ashby Ltd
10 Philips Lane, London EC3M 8AA
Tel: 01-626 8071, Telex: 886170

Associated Lead Manufacturers Ltd*
Clements House, 14-18 Gresham St,
London EC2P 2JS
Tel: 01-606 4400, Telex: 884141,
Cables: Associated London

Astra Metals & Residues Ltd
Northway House, High Rd, Whetstone,
London N20 9LP
Tel: 01-446 4381, Telex: 267401

Austral Metals Ltd
9 Park Place, St James's, London SW1A 1LX
Tel: 01-493 8474, Telex: 23672

Ayrton & Partners Ltd
Friendly House, 21-24 Chiswell St, London EC1Y 4SN
Tel: 01-638 5588, Telex: 887648

Bache Halsey Stuart (London) Ltd
Plantation House, Fenchurch St, London EC3M 3EP

Bassett Smith & Co Ltd
9 Harp Lane, Lower Thames St, London EC3R 6DR
Tel: 01-626 4533, Telex: 884754

Henry Bath & Son Ltd*
Market Bldgs, Mincing Lane, London EC3R 7DA
Tel: 01-626 1981, Telex: 887700,
Cables: Bathota

BICC Ltd
PO Box 1, Prescot, Merseyside L34 5SZ
Tel: 0772-426 6571, Telex: 627364

BICC Metals Ltd
PO Box 1, Prescot, Merseyside L34 5SZ
Tel: 0772-426 6571, Telex: 627364

Billiton-Enthoven Metals Ltd*
Colonial House, Mincing Lane, London EC3R 7DP
Tel: 01-623 2080, Telex: 887939

Billiton Metal & Ores (UK) Ltd
3-4 Lincolns Inn Fields, London WC2A 3AA
Tel: 01-831 7252, Telex: 885737

M C Brackenbury & Co
19 St Mary-at-Hill, London EC3R 8EE
Tel: 01-623 5701, 5707, Telex: 883304

Brandeis Goldschmidt & Co Ltd*
4 Fore St, London EC2P 2NU
Tel: 01-638 5877, Telex: 88401

Brittania Lead Co Ltd
Adelaide House, King William St,
London EC4R 9DX
Tel: 01-626 7446, Telex: 884210

British American Metals Co Ltd
French Railways House, 178-179 Piccadilly,
London W1V 0QH
Tel: 01-493 7835, Telex: 27380

Cerro Metals (UK) Ltd*
Pinners Hall, Austin Friars, London
EC2N 8BE
Tel: 01-628 5957, Telex: 887276,
Cables: Cerro UK

Chloride Metals Ltd
Felixstowe Rd, Abbey Wood,
London SE2 9RW
Tel: 01-310 4444, Telex: 896948

Cominco (UK) Ltd*
50 Finsbury Square, London EC2A 1DD
Tel: 01-638 4000, Telex: 886563,
Cables: Tadanac, London

The Commercial Metal Co Ltd*
Park House, 16 Finsubry Circus, London
EC2M 7DJ
Tel: 01-638 5789, Telex: 887410, 887419,
Cables: Cometalco

Commodity Analysis Ltd
37-39 St Andrews Hill, London EC4V 5DD
Tel: 01-248 9571, Telex: 883356

Congrain Metals Ltd
Creechurch House, Creechurch Lane,
London EC3A 5DR
Tel: 01-283 0111, Telex: 8812396

Conti Commodity Services Ltd
Europe House, World Trade Centre,
London E1 9AA
Tel: 01-488 3232, Telex: 887438,
Cables: TGR/CCSG

Continental Ore Europe Ltd*
18 Rood Lane, London EC3M 8BS
Tel: 01-623 3621, Telex: 886269

C Czarnikow Ltd
PO Box 602, 66 Mark Lane, London
EC3P 3EA
Tel: 01-480 6677, Telex: 885011

Charles Davis (Metal Brokers) Ltd*
5 Whittington Ave, London EC3V 1LE
Tel: 01-626 3538, Telex: 883928,
Cables: Losange

Delta Metal Co Ltd
1 Kingsway, London WC2B 6XF
Tel: 01-836 3535, Telex: 27762,
Cables: Delta Kings Ldn

Delta Metal Co Ltd
Greets Green Rd, West Bromwich,
West Midlands B70 9ER
Tel: 021-5536188, Telex: 33127,
Cables: Extrusion West Bromwich

Derby & Co Ltd
Moor House, London Wall, London EC2 5JE
Tel: 01-638 2876, Telex: 883801,
Cables: Plativet London EC2

Dietiker Metals (UK) Ltd
29 Throgmorton St, London EC2N 2AN
Tel: 01-638 0911, Telex: 887734/35,
Cables: Dmet UK

Drexel Burnham Lambert Ltd
Winchester House, 77 London Wall,
London EC2N 1BE
Tel: 01-628 3200, Telex: 884995, 884845,
Cables: Coburnham London EC2

Enfield Rolling Mills Ltd
Millmarsh Lane, Brimsdown, Enfield,
Jiddlesex
Tel: 01-804 1255, Telex: 22869,
Cables: Rolen-mil

Engelhard Sales Ltd
St Nicholas House, St Nicholas Rd, Sutton,
Surrey
Tel: 01-643 8080, Telex: 22317,
Cables: Platmetals, Sutton, Surrey

H J Enthoven & Sons Ltd
3-4 Lincoln's Inn Fields, London WC2A 3AA
Tel: 01-831 7252, Telex: 885737 BUK G

Entores (Metal Brokers) Ltd*
City Wall House, 79-83 Chiswell St,
London EC1Y 4TB
Tel: 01-606 6050, Telex: 887621

EZ Europe Ltd
9 Park Place, St James's, London SW1A 1LX
Tel: 01-629 1437, Telex: 23671

Frank Fehr & Co Ltd
Prince Rupert House, 64 Queen St,
London EC4R 1ER
Tel: 01-248 5066, Telex: 888960

Fergusson Wild & Co Ltd
3 St Helen's Place, London EC3A 6DB
Tel: 01-588 7022, Telex: 883503

Gardner Lohmann Ltd
6 Laurence Pountney Hill, London EC4R 0BL
Tel: 01-626 8086, Telex: 884458, 886388

Gerald Metals Ltd*
Europe House World Trade Centre,
St Katherine-by-the-Tower, London E1
Tel: 01-481 0681, Telex: 883869,
Cables: GMET London

Gill & Duffus Ltd*
St Dunstan's House, 201 Borough High St,
London SE1 1HW
Tel: 01-407 7050, Telex: 887588

Gill & Duffus (Metals) Ltd
St Dunstan's House, 201 Borough High St,
London SE1 1HW
Tel: 01-407 7050, Telex: 887588

M Golodetz Ltd
29 Mincing Lane, London EC3R 7EE
Tel: 01-626 4383, Telex: 855016

M Golodetz (Overseas) Ltd
Aldwych House, 71-91 Aldwych,
London WC2B 4HN
Tel: 01-242 8888, Telex: 23567,
Cables: Goloseas London WC2

Harlow & Jones Ltd
St Albans House, 59 Haymarket, London SW1
Tel: 01-839 8030, Telex: 917691,
Cables: Harjones

Heathfield Proprietary Ltd
9 Park Place, St James's, London SW1
Tel: 01-493 8474, Telex: 23672

IMI Ltd
PO Box 216, Kynoch Works, Witton,
Birmingham B6 7BA
Tel: 021-3564848, Telex: 366771,
Cables: Kynoch Birmingham

Imperial Chemical Industries Ltd
Imperial Chemical House, Millbank,
London SW1P 3JF
Tel: 01-834 4444, Telex: 21324,
Cables: Impkemix

Intsel Ltd*
4th Floor, 85 Gracechurch St, London
EC3V 0AA
Tel: 01-623 3691, Telex: 8811981,
Cables: Intsel London EC3

A C Israel Woodhouse Co Ltd
21 Mincing Lane, London EC3P 7DN
Tel: 01-623 3131, Telex: 88742,
Cables: Acicowood Ldn

Jacob Metals Ltd
8 Waterloo Place, St James's, London
SW1Y 4AH
Tel: 01-930 6953, Telex: 918034,
Cables: Metaljacob

Johnson Mathey Commodities Ltd
5 Lloyds Ave, London EC3N 3DB
Tel: 01-481 3181, Telex: 884312

Johnson & Nephew (Non-Ferrous) Ltd
Dale House, Tiviot Dale, Stockport SK1 1TP
Tel: 061-4775252, Telex: 667851

G W Joynson & Co Ltd
14 Trinity Square, London EC3N 4ES
Tel: 01-480 6921, Telex: 885346,
Cables: Warrior

Leopold Lazarus Ltd*
Gotch House, 20-34 St Bride St, London
EC4A 4DL
Tel: 01-583 8060, Telex: 265544,
Cables: Orminiaz

Leigh & Sillivan Group Ltd
Knights Pool, Windmill St, Macclesfield,
Cheshire SK11 7HR
Tel: 0625-31331, Telex: 688363,
Cables: Sillivan Macclesfield

Lewis & Peat (Metals) Ltd
32 St Mary-at-Hill, London EC3R 8DH
Tel: 01-623 3111, Telex: 883983

Lonconex Ltd*
29 Mincing Lane, London EC3R 7EU
Tel: 01-626 4383, Telex: 885016,
Cables: Lonconex London EC3

J Lowenstein & Co Ltd
Lometa House, 12-14 River Rd, Barking,
Essex 1G11 0DG
Tel: 01-591 1114, Telex: 897224,
Cables: Lometa

Mack Dix & Co Ltd
Plantation House, Mincing Lane,
London EC3M 3PH
Tel: 01-626 0101, Telex: 885977

MacLaine Watson & Co Ltd*
2-4 Idol Lane, London EC3R 5DL
Tel: 01-283 8611, Telex: 884328

Metallgesellschaft Ltd*
19-21 Gt Tower St, London EC3R 5AQ
Tel: 01-626 4221, Telex: 888971,
Cables: Metallbank London

Metal Scrap and By-Products Ltd
110 Queen Victoria St, London EC4V 4AU
Tel: 01-236 8931, Telex: 887151

Metdist Ltd*
Barrington House, 59-67 Gresham St,
London EC2V 7EY
Tel: 01-606 0463, Telex: 888248

Metro Metal Traders Ltd
Station House, Harrow Rd, Wembley
HA9 6DE
Tel: 01-903 4971, Telex: 923548

Moutafian Commodities Ltd
2-4 Eastcheap, London EC3M 1AL
Tel: 01-623 3311, Telex: 884412,
Cables: Moutafian London

Noranda Sales Corp of Canada Ltd
New Zealand House, Haymarket,
London SW1Y 4TH
Tel: 01-839 7601, Telex: 24666,
Cables: Noranda, London

Jeremy Oates Ltd
16 Monument St, London EC3R 8AJ
Tel: 01-623 7301, Telex: 888264

Pacol Ltd
47 Mark Lane, London EC3R 7QX
Tel: 01-623 1000, Telex: 888712,
Cables: Pacolanter

Philipp & Lion*
Moor House, London Wall, London
EC2Y 5AR
Tel: 01-678 3060, Telex: 888555

Pirelli General Cable Works Ltd
PO Box 4, Western Esplanade,
Southampton SO9 7AE
Tel: 0703-20381, Telex: 47522

J H Rayner (Mincing Lane) Ltd*
50 Mark Lane, London EC3R 7RJ
Tel: 01-709 9144, Telex: 883461

Marc Rich & Co Ltd
49 Wigmore St, London W1H 9LE
Tel: 01-935 4455, Telex: 21223/4

Richmond Metal Co Ltd
Dellbow Rd, North Feltham Trading Estate,
Faggs Rd, Feltham, Middlesex
Tel: 01-890 0981, Telex: 934857

Henry Rogers (London) Ltd
9 Harp Lane, Great Tower St, London
EC3R 6DP
Tel: 01-626 4533, Telex: 884724

Sharps, Pixley Ltd*
10 Rood Lane, London EC3M 8BB
Tel: 01-623 8000, Telex: 883319

Shearson Hayden Stone Ltd
St Alphage House, 2 Fore St, London
EC2Y 5DA
Tel: 01-588 7505, Telex: 888881

Sogemin (Metals) Ltd*
10th Floor, Stock Exchange Building,
Throgmorton St, London EC2N 1EL
Tel: 01-628 6421, Telex: 885244

Tennant Trading (Metals) Ltd*
9 Harp Lane, Lower Thames St, London
EC3R 6DR
Tel: 01-626 4533, Telex: 887604

H P Thompson & Sons Ltd*
8 Lloyds Ave, London EC3N 3AB
Tel: 01-480 7951, Telex: 8951635,
Cables: Knilomet London EC3

Triland Metals Ltd*
Bow Bells House, Bread St, London
EC4M 9BQ
Tel: 01-236 5551, Telex: 888677,
Cables: Trimet, London EC4

Wallace Brothers Commodities Ltd
108 Fenchurch St, London EC3M 5HP
Tel: 01-481 8671, Telex: 887442

H A Watson & Co Ltd
11 Mansfield Rd, Rotherham, Yorkshire
Tel: 0709-74293, Telex: 547393

Westralian Ores and Metals Ltd
15 Blackfriars Lane, London EC4V 6ER
Tel: 01-248 5987, Telex: 887444

Wilson Smithett and Cope*
32 St Mary-at-Hill, London EC3R 8DH
Tel: 01-623 9333, Telex: 883898,
Cables: Infados

Woodhouse Drake and Carey Ltd
Three Quays, Tower Hill, London EC3R 6EP
Tel: 01-623 7575, Telex: 886271,
Cables: Progne

Rudolf Wolff and Co Ltd*
Knollys House, 11 Byward St, London
EC3R 5ED
Tel: 01-626 8765, Telex: 885034,
Cables: Occasion, London

Appendix 6:

London gold market members

Derby & Company Ltd
Moor House
London Wall
London EC2Y 5JE
United Kingdom
Tel: 01-638 2876

Johnson Matthey (Bankers) Ltd
5 Lloyds Avenue
London EC3
United Kingdom
Tel: 01-481 3181

Mocatta & Goldsmid Ltd
16 Finsbury Circus
London EC2
United Kingdom
Tel: 01-638 3636/2825

Rothschild, N M & Sons Ltd
New Court
St Swithins Lane
London EC4
United Kingdom
Tel: 01-626 4356

Samuel Montagu & Co Ltd
114 Old Broad Street
London EC2
United Kingdom
Tel: 01-588 6464

Sharps Pixley Ltd
34 Lime Street
London EC3
United Kingdom
Tel: 01-623 8000

Appendix 7:
Acceptable Melters and Assayers

The following list shows melters and assayers whose marks are recognized and accepted by the London Gold Market.

Great Britain	Most Recent Marks
Engelhard Industries Ltd	Engelhard London, and 'E'
Daniel C. Griffith & Co Ltd *Assayers only*	Assay Certificate only
Johnson Matthey Chemicals Ltd	Johnson Matthey London Refiners, and assay mark
The Sheffield Smelting Co Ltd	Refined by The Sheffield Smelting Co Ltd London & Sheffield, and assay mark
Australia	
Engelhard Industries Pty Ltd	Refined by Engelhard Industries Pty Ltd, Australia, and assay mark
Matthey Garret Pty Ltd, formerly Garrett, Davidson & Matthey Pty Ltd	Matthey Garrett Pty Ltd, Sydney Refiners, and assay mark
The Perth Mint, formerly the Perth branch of The Royal Mint, London	The Perth Mint, and mint mark
Belgium	
Johnson Matthey & Pauwels SA	Johnson Matthey & Pauwels Bruxelles Brussel, and assay mark
N.V. Métallurgie Hoboken-Overpelt SA, formerly Métallurgie Hoboken SA and Société Générale Métallurgique de Hoboken	Métallurgie Hoboken-Overpelt, and individual assayer's mark
Canada	
Canadian Copper Refiners Ltd	Refined (year) Canadian Copper Refiners Ltd, Montreal East Canada
Engelhard Industries of Canada Ltd	Engelhard, with trade mark
Johnson Matthey & Mallory Ltd	Johnson Matthey & Mallory Canada, and assay mark
Royal Canadian Mint	Royal Canadian Mint
China, People's Republic of	
Refinery of China	Refined by Refinery of China Peking, and assay mark (English and Chinese script)

France
In France the assay stamps used are those registered by individual Assayers with the Chambre Syndicale des Agents de Change.

Caplain Saint-André SA	Caplain Saint-André Affineurs-Fondeurs Paris, and individual assayer's mark

Compagnie des Métaux Précieux	Compagnie des Métaux Précieux Paris Fondeurs Fondeurs Affineurs, and individual assayer's mark
Comptoir Lyon-Alemand-Louyot	Comptoir-Lyon-Alemand, Louyot-Paris Affineur Fondeur, and individual assayer's mark
Laboratoires Boudet & Dussaix	Fondu Par Laboratoires Boudet & Dussaix, and individual assayer's mark
Les Anciens Etablissements Léon Martin, formerly Etablissements Léon Martin	Anc Ets Léon Martin Fondeur Affineur Bagneux Près Paris, and individual assayer's mark
Germany, Federal Republic of	
*Deutsche Gold-und Silber-Scheideanstalt Vormals Roessler	DEGUSSA, and trade mark
W C Heraeus GmbH	Heraeus Edelmetalle GmbH Hanau
*Norddeutsche Affinerie	Norddeutsche Affinerie Hamburg, and 'NA'
Italy	
Metalli Preziosi SpA	MP Metalli Preziosi SpA Milano, Affinazione Consociata Italiana Johnson Matthey & Co Ltd, London, and assay mark
Korea, Democratic People's Republic of	
Central Bank, DPR of Korea	Central Bank Pyongyang Refiners Melters, Central Bank DPR of Korea, and assay mark
Netherlands	
H. Drijfhout & Zoon's Edelmetaalbedrijven BV, formerly H. Drijfhout & Zoon's Edelmetaalbedrijven NV	H. Drijfhout & Zoon Amsterdam Melters, and assay mark
Schöne Edelmetaal BV, formerly Schönes Essaieer-Inrichting en Handel in Edele Metalen NV	Guaranteed by Schöne NV Amsterdam, and brand mark
Romania, Socialist Republic of	
National Bank of the Socialist Republic of Romania *Assayers only*	Banca Nationala A Republicii Socialiste Romania
Uzinele metalurgice de metale neferoase *Melters only*	Uzinele metalurgice de metale neferoase Baia-Mare
South Africa, Republic of	
Rand Refinery Ltd	Rand Refinery Ltd, trade mark and assay mark
Spain	
Industrias Reunidas Minero-Metalurgicas, SA (Indumetal)	Indumetal, and Orispania Bilbao
Switzerland	
Argor SA	Argor SA Chiasso, and assay mark
Métaux Précieux SA	Métaux Précieux SA Neuchatel, and assay mark
Usine Genevoise de Dégrossissage d'Or	UGDO Essayeur Fondeur
Valcambi SA	Valcambi SA Balerna-Suisse, and assay mark
US	
ASARCO Inc, formerly American Smelting & Refining Company	Asarco Gold Amarillo Texas or Gold Asarco Baltimore Maryland or Gold Asarco Perth Amboy New Jersey
Engelhard Minerals & Chemicals Corporation Engelhard Industries Division	Engelhard New Jersey US or 'E', with an assay mark of 'EI'

**Bearing the date stamp 1953 and onwards*

Handy & Harman	Handy & Harman
Homestake Mining Company	Homestake Mining Company (must be as a logo stamp)
United States Assay Offices & Mints	U.S. Assay Office New York, or Mint of The United States at San Francisco, or US Mint San Francisco, or US Mint Denver
United States Metals Refining Company Subsidiary of AMAX Inc	DRW Reg US Pat Off
USSR	
State Refineries	CCCP, with hammer and sickle

Former Melters and Assayers

The following organizations no longer melt or assay good delivery bars. However, bars produced by them in the past continue to be accepted by Members of the Market.

United Kingdom	**Marks**
Bank of England	Bank of England with Britannia seated holding spear
Johnson & Sons, Assayers, Ltd *Assayers only*	Assay Office stamp
Johnson & Sons' Smelting Works Ltd	Johnson & Sons' Smelting Works Refiners Melters
Johnson, Matthey & Co, Ltd Authority transferred to Johnson Matthey Chemicals Ltd	Johnson Matthey London Refiners Melters, and assay mark (and earlier styles)
N M Rothschild & Sons	N M Rothschild & Sons RMR
The Royal Mint	Coat of Arms of The Royal Mint
Australia	
Former Australian Branches of The Royal Mint, London	Royal Mint Perth Branch, and mint mark Royal Mint Melbourne, and mint mark
France	
Comptoir Lyon-Alemand, Louyot SA, formerly Comptoir Lyon-Alemand Louyot & Cie	Comptoir Lyon-Alemand, Louyot & Cie Paris Affineurs-Fondeurs, and individual assayer's mark
Comptoir Lyon-Alemand et Marret, Bonnin, Lebel et Guieu réunis	Comptoir Lyon-Alemand et Marret Bonnin Lebel et Guieu réunis, and individual assayer's mark
Comptoir Lyon-Alemand *Melters only*	Comptoir Lyon-Alemand, and individual assayer's mark
Marret, Bonnin, Lebel et Guieu *Melters only*	Marret, Bonnin, Lebel et Guieu, and individual assayer's mark
Switzerland	
Bureau Central Suisse, Contrôle Métaux Précieux *Assayers only*	Bureau Central Suisse, Contrôle Métaux Précieux
Monnaie Federale Suisse *Melters only*	Monnaie Federale Suisse
Société de Banque Suisse	Société de Banque Suisse Le Lôcle, and assay mark

Appendix 8:

Gold bullion dealers and gold bankers

J Aron & Co Inc
160 Water Street
New York
NY 10038
United States
Tel: 212-7575 300

Bank Leu
32 Bahnhofstrasse
8022 Zurich
Switzerland
Tel: 411-219 1111

Credit Suisse
Postfach
8021 Zurich
Switzerland
Tel: 411-215 1111

Deutsche Bank Ag
Postfach 2623
6000 Frankfurt 1
West Germany
Tel: 611-2141

Dresdner Bank
Gallusanlage 7-8
6000 Frankfurt 1
West Germany
Tel: 611-2631

Johnson Matthey (Bankers) Ltd
5 Lloyds Avenue
London EC3
United Kingdom
Tel: 01-481 3181

Mocatta & Goldsmid
16 Finsbury Circus
London EC2
United Kingdom
Tel: 01-638 3636/2825

Mocatta Metals
4 World Trade Center
Suite 5200
New York
NY 10048
United States
Tel: 212-9389 600

Samuel Montagu
114 Old Broad Street
London EC2
United Kingdom
Tel: 01-588 6464

Republic National Bank
452 5th Avenue
New York
United States
Tel: 212-930 6000

Rothschild N M & Sons Ltd
New Court
St Swithins Lane
London EC4
United Kingdom
Tel: 01-626 4356 Telex: 888031

Sharps Pixley Ltd
34 Lime Street
London EC3
United Kingdom
Tel: 01-623 8000

Swiss Bank
Aeschenvorstadt 1
4002 Basle
Switzerland
Tel: 4161-202 020

Union Bank of Switzerland
45 Bahnhofstrasse
8021 Zurich
Switzerland
Tel: 411-234 1111

Appendix 9:
Major gold fabricating firms

Degussa
Postfach 2644
D-6000 Frankfurt 1
West Germany
Tel: 49611-2181

Englehard Industries
299 Park Avenue
New York
NY 10017
United States
Tel: 212-7643 700

Gori & Zucchi SpA
Via Fiorentina 550
52100 Arezzo
Italy
Tel: 350851 Telex: 570060

Handy & Harman
850 Third Avenue
New York
NY 10022
United States
Tel: 212-752 3400

Johnson Matthey & Co
5 Lloyds Avenue
London EC3
United Kingdom
Tel: 01-481 3181

Comptoir Lyon Alemand Louyot
13 rue Montmorency
75139 Paris
France
Tel: 331-27 71 111

Appendix 10:
Dealers in precious metals

Alphamet International
Division of Franco-Suisse SA
25-27 Avenue de Villiers
75017 Paris
France
Tel: 331-766-53 40 Telex: 641830

AMAX Copper Inc
1270 Avenue of the Americas
New York
NY 10017
United States

Argos Metals Ltd
140 Park Lane
London W1Y 4AD
United Kingdom
Tel: 01-629 4116 Telex: 886732

J Aron
160 Water Street
New York
NY 10038
United States

ASARCO Inc
120 Broadway
New York
NY 10005
United States

Ayrton Metals Ltd
Imperial House
Dominion Street
London EC2M 2SD
United Kingdom
Tel: 01-638 9731 Telex: 883908

Bache Halsey Stuart Inc
100 Gold Street
New York
NY 10038
United States

Behr Metals
Division of Joseph Behr & Sons Inc
1100 Seminary Avenue
Rockford
Illinois 61108
United States

Boliden Aktiebolag
Sturegatan 22
Box 5508
S-11485 Stockholm
Sweden

Brandeis Goldschmidt & Co Inc
919 Third Avenue
New York
NY 10022
United States

The Broken Hill Associated
Smelters Pty Ltd
Melbourne 3001
Australia

The Bunker Hill Co
477 Madison Avenue
Suite 2400
New York
NY 10022
United States

Capper Pass & Son Ltd
North Ferriby
North Humberside
United Kingdom

Cerro Sales Corp
300 Park Avenue
New York
NY 10022
United States

Cie des Métaux Précieux
56 Rue de Turbigo
Paris 3
France
Tel 331-277 71 10

Commodity Analysis Ltd
37-39 St Andrews Hill
London EC4V 5DD
United Kingdom
Tel: 01-248 9571 Telex: 883356

Commodity Exchange Inc
4 World Trade Center
New York
NY 10048
United States
Tel: 212-938 2900

Continental Gold Corp
820 Second Avenue
New York
NY 10017
United States
Tel: 212-421 9811

Credita Minero y Mercantil SA
Paseco de la Reforma
No 144 Mexico 6
DF Mexico

Degussa
Postfach 2644
D-6000
Frankfurt 1
West Germany
Tel: 49611-2181

Diversified Industries
123 Byassee Drive
Hazelwood
Montana 63042
United States

Englehard Minerals & Chemicals Corp
430 Mountain Avenue
Murray Hill
NJ 07974
United States

Falconbridge International Ltd
7 King Street
E Toronto
Canada

Federated Metals Corp
120 Broadway
New York
NY 10005
United States

Gerald Metals Inc
1 Battery Park
New York
NY 10044
United States
Tel: 212-425 4160

Gerald Metals Ltd
World Trade Centre
St Katherine-by-the-Tower
London E1
United Kingdom
Tel: 01-481 0681 Telex: 884377

Giuliano Staccioli Metalli
Preziosi SpA
Via S Sebastianello 9
00187 Rome
Italy

D F Goldsmith Chemical
& Metal Corp
909 Pitner Avenue
Evanston
Illinois 60202
United States

Gray International Inc
1271 Avenue of the Americas
New York
NY 10020
United States
Tel: 212-581 2226

Handy & Harman
850 Third Avenue
New York
NY 10022
United States
Tel: 212-752 3400

Homeslake Mining Co
650 California Street
San Francisco
California 94108
United States

Hudson Bay Mining
& Smelting Co Ltd
Toronto-Dominion Center
Toronto
Canada

Indium Corporation of America
PO Box 269
Utica
New York
NY 13603
United States

Indussa Corp
1212 Avenue of the Americas
New York
NY 10036
United States

Johnson Matthey Bankers Ltd
5 Lloyds Avenue
London EC3
United Kingdom
Tel: 01-481 3181

Kennecott Sales Corp
161 East 42nd Street
New York
NY 10017
United States

Kinsho-Mataichi Corp
80 Pine Street
New York
NY 10005
United States

Leytess Metal & Chemical Corp
500 5th Avenue
New York
NY 10036
United States
Tel: 212-564 1915

Lissner Corp
1000 N Branch Street
Chicago
Illinois 60672
United States

Martin Metals Inc
1321 Wilson Street
Los Angeles
California 90021
United States

Matthey Bishop Inc
Malvern
Pennsylvania 19355
United States

Metal Traders Inc
445 Park Avenue
New York
NY 10022
United States

Minemet Metals Inc
450 Park Avenue
New York
NY 10022
United States

Mitsui Mining & Smelting Co Ltd
2-1 Muromachi
Chuo-ku
Tokyo
Japan

Mocatta Metals Corp
25 Broad Street
New York
NY 10004
United States
Tel: 212-785 1222

Newmont Mining Corp
300 Park Avenue
New York
NY 10022
United States

The Ore & Chemical Corp
235 East 42nd Street
New York
NY 10017
United States

Oxy Metal Industries
85 River Road
Nutley
NJ 07110
United States

PGP-Industries Inc
Sub of Gerald Metals Inc
13429 Alondra Boulevard
Santa Fe Springs
California 90670
United States

Phelps Dodge Sales Co Inc
300 Park Avenue
New York
NY 10022
United States

Philipp Brothers Division of
Engelhard Minerals & Chemicals Corp
299 Park Avenue
New York
NY 10017
United States

Philipp Brothers
1221 Avenue of the Americas
New York
NY 10020
United States
Tel: 212-575 5900

Powell Metals & Chemicals Inc
1122 Milford Avenue
Rockford
Illinois 61125
United States
Tel: 815-963 3595

Precious Metals Refining Co Inc
826 North 3rd Street
Philadelphia
Pennsylvania 19123
United States

Republic National Bank
of New York
452 Fifth Avenue
New York
NY 10018
United States

Reynolds Metals Co
6801 W Broad Street
Richmond
Virginia 23261
United States

Redman & Yaruss Refining Co Inc
17 West 47th Street
New York
NY 10036
United States

Sabin Metal Corp
316-334 Meserole Street
Brooklyn
NY 10006
United States

J A Samuel & Co Inc
233 Broadway
New York
NY 10007
United States

Simmons Refining Co Inc
1708 S Normal Avenue
Chicago
Illinois 60616
United States

SIPI Metals Corp
1720 N Elston Avenue
Chicago
Illinois 60622
United States

Sifkin Smelting & Refining Inc
PO Box 708
Lewistown
Pennsylvania 17044
United States

Strauss International Corp
450 Seventh Avenue
New York
NY 10001
United States

Sulsman & Blumenthal Inc
500 Flatbush Avenue
Hartford
Connecticut 06103
United States

SUPPO Smelting & Refining Co Inc
1240 W Carroll Avenue
Chicago
Illinois 60607
United States

Troy Metals
5546 Satsuma Avenue
North Hollywood
California 91601
United States

United Mineral & Chemical Corp
129 Hudson Street
New York
NY 10013
United States

United Refining & Smelting Co
3700 N Runge Avenue
Franklin Park
Illinois 60131
United States

Appendix 11:

Conversion of US metal prices from cents per lb to sterling pounds per metric ton* at varying exchange rates

Metal price: cents per lb	Exchange rate: US dollar/£ sterling 1.50	1.60	1.70	1.80	1.90	2.00	2.10	2.20	2.30	2.40
					£ sterling per metric ton					
1	14.69	13.77	12.96	12.24	11.60	11.02	10.49	10.01	9.58	9.18
5	73.46	68.85	64.80	61.20	58.00	55.10	52.45	50.05	47.91	45.91
10	146.93	137.70	129.60	122.40	116.00	110.20	104.90	100.10	95.82	91.83
20	293.86	275.40	259.20	244.80	232.00	220.40	209.80	200.20	191.64	183.66
30	440.79	413.10	388.80	367.20	348.00	330.60	314.70	300.30	287.46	275.49
40	587.72	550.80	518.40	489.60	464.00	440.80	419.60	400.40	383.28	367.32
50	734.65	688.50	648.00	612.00	580.00	551.00	524.50	500.50	479.10	459.15
60	881.58	826.20	777.60	734.40	696.00	661.20	629.40	600.60	574.92	550.98
70	1,028.51	963.90	907.20	856.80	812.00	771.40	734.30	700.70	670.74	642.81
80	1,175.44	1,101.60	1,036.80	979.20	928.00	881.60	839.20	800.80	766.56	734.64
90	1,322.37	1,239.30	1,166.40	1,101.60	1,044.00	991.80	944.10	900.90	862.38	826.47
100	1,469.30	1,377.00	1,296.00	1,224.00	1,160.00	1,102.00	1,049.00	1,001.00	958.20	918.30

* *metric ton = 2,204 lbs*

Appendix 12:

Average monthly dollar/sterling rate based on the market price at 11.30 a.m. each dealing day

	January	February	March	April	May	June	July	August	Sept-ember	Oc-tober	Nov-ember	Dec-ember	Average
1958	2.8000	2.8000	2.8000	2.8000	2.8000	2.7999	2.7979	2.7978	2.7981	2.7980	2.7995	2.7994	**2.7992**
1959	2.8047	2.8077	2.8103	2.8148	2.8127	2.8109	2.8101	2.8080	2.8020	2.8050	2.8012	2.7970	**2.8070**
1960	2.7985	2.8017	2.8041	2.8078	2.8046	2.8010	2.8065	2.8084	2.8107	2.8096	2.8119	2.8057	**2.8059**
1961	2.8047	2.7986	2.7956	2.7965	2.7922	2.7888	2.7854	2.8006	2.8096	2.8136	2.8130	2.8078	**2.8005**
1962	2.8089	2.8126	2.8132	2.8122	2.8105	2.8068	2.8050	2.8023	2.7995	2.7999	2.8001	2.8019	**2.8061**
1963	2.8031	2.8018	2.7990	2.7990	2.7980	2.7986	2.7993	2.7981	2.7961	2.7964	2.7964	2.7951	**2.7984**
1964	2.7967	2.7955	2.7966	2.7974	2.7979	2.7926	2.7884	2.7852	2.7819	2.7820	2.7833	2.7887	**2.7905**
1965	2.7895	2.7932	2.7904	2.7938	2.7953	2.7904	2.7892	2.7891	2.7945	2.8014	2.8020	2.8003	**2.7941**
1966	2.8025	2.8010	2.7938	2.7918	2.7908	2.7884	2.7873	2.7875	2.7877	2.7901	2.7896	2.7884	**2.7916**
1967	2.7892	2.7924	2.7943	2.7974	2.7952	2.7899	2.7860	2.7838	2.7829	2.7817	2.6430	2.4062	**2.7452**
1968	2.4087	2.4094	2.3992	2.4015	2.3891	2.3845	2.3892	2.3912	2.3869	2.3895	2.3874	2.3838	**2.3934**
1969	2.3866	2.3910	2.3913	2.3928	2.3862	2.3896	2.3902	2.3855	2.3837	2.3896	2.3962	2.3967	**2.3900**
1970	2.3999	2.4042	2.4056	2.4059	2.4033	2.3976	2.3903	2.3877	2.3845	2.3870	2.3899	2.3903	**2.3955**
1971	2.4047	2.4170	2.4182	2.4175	2.4183	2.4179	2.4182	2.4342	2.4709	2.4915	2.4937	2.5267	**2.4441**
1972	2.5703	2.6030	2.6178	2.6093	2.6117	2.5814	2.4415	2.4502	2.4425	2.3968	2.3518	2.3456	**2.5018**
1973	2.3558	2.4418	2.4778	2.4825	2.5174	2.5743	2.5402	2.4742	2.4163	2.4260	2.3890	2.3171	**2.4510**
1974	2.2263	2.2738	2.3369	2.3906	2.4117	2.3876	2.3869	2.3445	2.3146	2.3310	2.3271	2.3271	**2.3382**
1975	2.3603	2.3917	2.4172	2.3680	2.3185	2.2807	2.1833	2.1133	2.0852	2.0548	2.0499	2.0208	**2.2203**
1976	2.0276	2.0257	1.9455	1.8476	1.8156	1.7710	1.7863	1.7819	1.7309	1.6401	1.6370	1.6787	**1.8073**
1977	1.7127	1.7100	1.7172	1.7195	1.7188	1.7193	1.7221	1.7403	1.7436	1.7703	1.8203	1.8550	**1.7458**
1978	1.9338	1.9405	1.9103	1.8507	1.8175	1.8366	1.8940	1.9419	1.9593	—	—	—	—

Appendix 13:

Conversion table

Mass	Metric ton	Long ton	Short ton	Pounds	Kilograms	Ounce troy	Grains	Pennyweight	Pikul
Metric ton		0.984	1.102	2204.5	1000				16.535
Long ton	1.016		1.120	2240	1016				
Short ton	0.907	0.893		2000	907				15.000
Pound	0.0004	0.0004	0.0005		0.4536	14.583	7000		
Kilogram	0.001			2.2045		32.150			
Ounce troy							480	20	
Grain						480			
Pennyweight							24		
Pikul	0.0605		0.067	133.33	60.48				

Appendix 14:
World time zones

Standard Times at noon Greenwich Mean Time

British Summer Time, which is one hour ahead of GMT, is observed from 02.00 hours on the third Sunday in March until 02.00 on the fourth Sunday in October. USA Daylight Saving Time, which is one hour ahead of local standard time, is observed in all states except Arizona, Hawaii and Michigan from 02.00 on the last Sunday in April until 02.00 on the last Sunday in October. In France, in 1977, Summer Time, which is also one hour ahead of local standard time, is observed from 24.00 hours on 3 April to 24.00 on 25 September.

Accra	12.00	Damascus	14.00	Ottawa	07.00
Adelaide	21.30	Darwin	21.30	Panama	07.00
Algiers	13.00	Delhi	17.30	Paris	13.00
Amman	14.00	Djakarta	20.00	Peking	20.00
Amsterdam	13.00	Dublin	12.00	Perth	20.00
Ankara	14.00	Gibraltar	13.00	Prague	13.00
Athens	14.00	Helsinki	14.00	Quebec	07.00
Auckland	24.00	Hobart	22.00	Rangoon	18.30
Baghdad	15.00	Hong Kong	20.00	Rawalpindi	17.00
Bangkok	19.00	Istanbul	14.00	Reykjavik	12.00
Beirut	14.00	Jerusalem	14.00	Rio de Janeiro	09.00
Belgrade	13.00	Karachi	17.00	Rome	13.00
Berlin	13.00	Kuala Lumpur	20.00	San Francisco	04.00
Berne	13.00	Lagos	13.00	Santiago	08.00
Bombay	17.30	Leningrad	15.00	Sofia	14.00
Bonn	13.00	Lima	07.00	Singapore	19.30
Brisbane	22.00	Lisbon	13.00	Stockholm	13.00
Brussels	13.00	Luxembourg	13.00	Sydney	22.00
Bucharest	14.00	Madras	17.30	Tehran	15.30
Budapest	13.00	Madrid	13.00	Tokyo	21.00
Buenos Aires	09.00	Melbourne	22.00	Toronto	07.00
Cairo	14.00	Mexico City	06.00	Tunis	13.00
Calcutta	17.30	Montevideo	08.30	Vancouver	04.00
Canberra	22.00	Moscow	15.00	Vienna	13.00
Cape Town	14.00	Nairobi	15.00	Warsaw	13.00
Caracas	08.00	New York	07.00	Washington	07.00
Chicago	06.00	Nicosia	14.00	Wellington	24.00
Copenhagen	13.00	Oslo	13.00	Winnipeg	06.00

Note to World Time Zones map
The earth turns one complete revolution in 24 hours. The surface of the Earth is divided into 24 Time Zones, each of 15° longitude or 1 hour of time. In 24 hours it turns through 360°. The times shown are the standard times on land and sea when it is 12.00 hours on the Greenwich Meridian.

World Time Zones

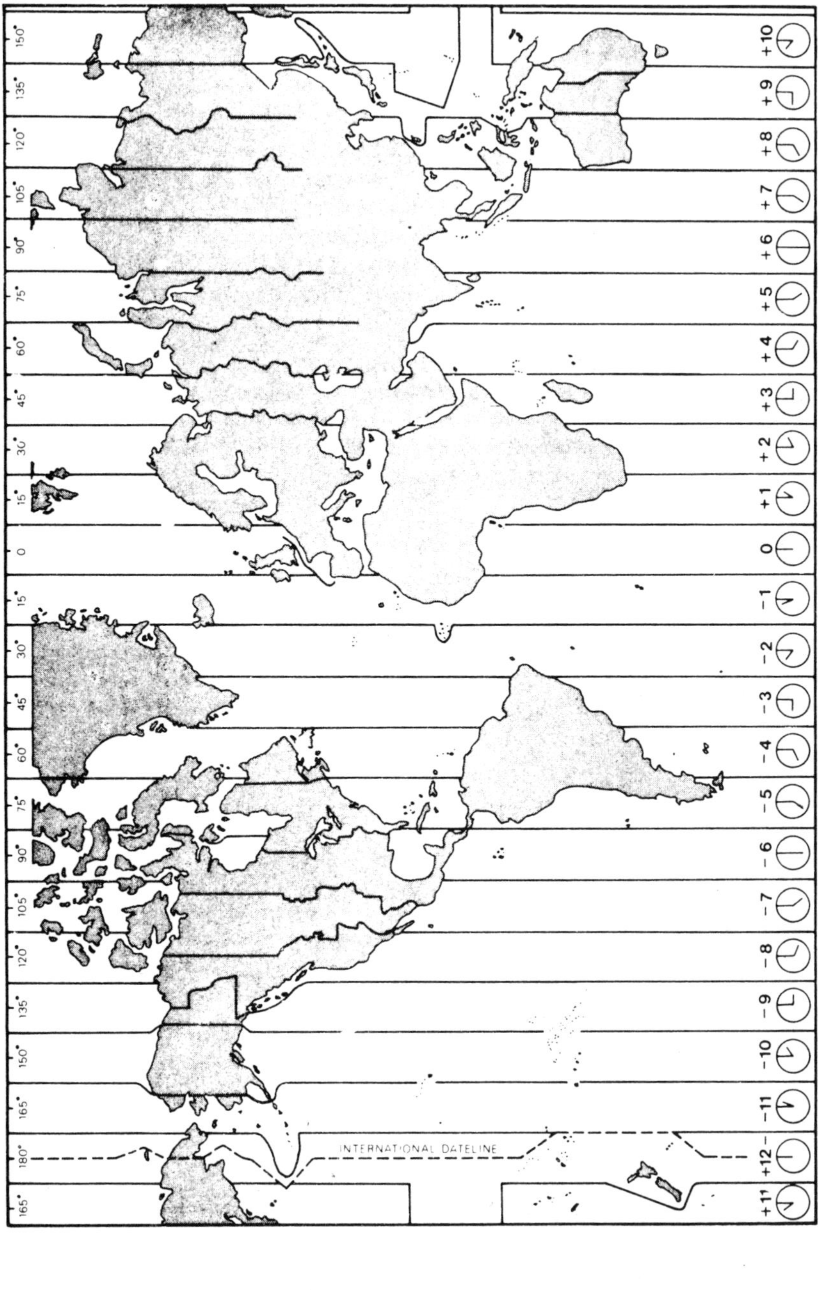

Appendix 15:
World currencies

Country	Basic or principal unit of currency
Afghanistan	Afghani
Albania	Lekë
Algeria	Algerian Dinar
Angola	Kwanza
Antigua	East Caribbean Dollar (EC$)
Argentina	Argentinian Peso
Australia	Australian Dollar
Austria	Schilling
Bahamas, The	Bahamian Dollar (BS)
Bahrain	Bahrain Dinar
Bangladesh	Taka
Barbados	East Caribbean Dollar (EC$)
Belgium	Belgian Franc
Belize	Belizean Dollar
Benin	Franc CFA
Bermuda	Bermudan Dollar (Canadian, UK and US currencies also in use)
Bhutan	Tikchung
Bolivia	Bolivian Peso
Botswana	Pula
Brazil	Cruzeiro
Brunei	Brunei Dollar
Bulgaria	Lev
Burma	Kyat
Burundi	Burundi Franc
Cameroun Republic	Franc de la Communauté Financière Africaine (Franc CFA)
Canada	Canadian Dollar
Central African Empire	Franc CFA
Central American Common Market	Central American Peso
Chad	Franc CFA
Chile	Chilean Escudo

Country	Basic or principal unit of currency
China, People's Republic of	Renminbi Yuan
Colombia	Colombian Peso
Congo (Brazzaville)	Franc CFA
Costa Rica	Colon
Cuba	Cuban Peso
Cyprus	Cyprus Pound
Czechoslovakia	Koruna
Dahomey	Franc CFA
Denmark	Danish Krone
Dominica	East Caribbean Dollar (EC$)
Dominican Republic	Dominican Republic Peso
Ecuador	Sucre
Egypt	Egyptian Pound (£E)
El Salvador	El Salvador Colon
Ethiopia	Ethiopian Birr
Fiji	Fijian Dollar $F)
Finland	Markka
France	French Franc
French Guinea	French Franc
Gabon	Franc CFA
Gambia	Dalasi
German Democratic Republic	Ostmark or DDR-Mark
Germany, Federal Republic	Deutsche Mark (DM)
Ghana	Cedi
Gibraltar	Gibraltar Pound
Greece	Drachma
Grenada	East Caribbean Dollar (EC$)
Guadeloupe	French Franc
Guatemala	Quetzal
Guinea-Bissau	Escudo
Guinea, Equatorial	Guinean Peseta
Guinea, Republic of	Sili
Guyana	Guyanese Dollar $G)
Haiti	Gourde
Honduras	Lempira (L)
Hong Kong	Hong Kong Dollar (HK$)
Hungary	Forint
Iceland	Icelandic Krona
India	Indian Rupee
Indonesia	Rupiah (Rp)
Iran	Iranian Rial
Iraq	Iraqi Dinar

Country	Basic or principal unit of currency
Ireland	Irish Pound
Israel	Israeli Pound (I£)
Italy	Lira
Ivory Coast	Franc CFA
Jamaica	Jamaican Dollar (J$)
Japan	Yen
Jordan	Jordanian Dinar (JD)
Kenya	Kenya Shilling (Ks)
Khmer Republic	Riel
Korea, Democratic People's Republic of (North Korea)	Won
Korea, Republic of (South Korea)	Won
Kuwait	Kuwait Dinar (KD)
Laos	Kip Pot Poi
Lebanon	Lebanese Pound (£L)
Lesotho	South African Rand
Liberia	Liberian Dollar (also US Dollar)
Libya	Libyan Dinar (LD)
Liechtenstein	Franken or Swiss Franc
Luxemburg	Luxemburg Franc
Macao	Pataca
Malagasy Republic	Franc Malgache (FMG)
Malawi	Kwacha (K)
Malaysia	Ringgit
Mali	Mali Franc
Malta	Maltese Pound
Martinique	Local Franc
Mauritania	Ouguiya
Mauritius	Mauritian Rupee
Mexico	Mexican Peso
Monaco	French Franc
Mongolia	Tugrik
Montserrat	East Caribbean Dollar (EC$)
Morocco	Dirham
Mozambique	Escudo
Namibia (South West Africa)	South African Rand
Nepal	Nepali Rupee (NR)
Netherlands	Netherlands Gulden or Guilder or Florin
Netherlands Antilles	Netherlands Antilles Florin (NAFl) or Guilder
New Zealand	New Zealand Dollar ($NZ)

Country	Basic or principal unit of currency
Nicaragua	Cordoba
Niger	Franc CFA
Nigeria	Naira
Norway	Norwegian Krone
Oman	Ryal Omani
Pakistan	Pakistan Rupee
Panama	Balboa
Papua New Guinea	Kina
Paraguay	Guarani
Peru	Gold Sol
Philippines	Philippine Peso
Pitcairn Islands	Australian Dollar
Poland	Zloty
Portugal	Portuguese Escudo
Puerto Rico	US Dollar ($)
Qatar	Qatar/Dubai Ryal
Réunion	French Franc
Rhodesia	Rhodesian Dollar (R$)
Romania	Leu
Rwanda	Rwanda Franc
St Kitts	East Caribbean Dollar (EC$)
St Lucia	East Caribbean Dollar (EC$)
St Vincent	East Caribbean Dollar (EC$)
Samoa (Western)	Tala
Saudi Arabia	Saudi Arabian Ryal
Senegal	Franc CFA
Seychelles	Rupee
Sierra Leone	Leone
Sikkim	Indian Rupee
Singapore	Singapore Dollar (S$)
Somalia	Somali Shilling
South Africa, Republic of	Rand (R)
South West Africa (Namibia)	South African Rand
Spain	Spanish Peseta
Sri Lanka	Sri Lanka Rupee
Sudan	Sudanese Pound
Surinam	Surinam Guilder (also Netherlands currency)
Swaziland	Lilangeni
Sweden	Swedish Krona
Switzerland	Franken or Swiss Franc
Syria	Syrian Pound (£S)

Country	Basic or principal unit of currency
Taiwan	New Taiwan Dollar
Tanzania	Tanzanian Shilling
Thailand	Baht
Togo	Franc CFA
Tonga	Pa'anga
Trinidad and Tobago	Trinidad and Tobago Dollar
Tunisia	Tunisian Dinar
Turkey	Turkish Lira (TL)
Uganda	Ugandan Shilling
United Arab Emirates	Dirham
United Kingdom (UK)	Pound Sterling (£)
United States of America (USA)	US Dollar ($)
Upper Volta	Franc CFA
Uruguay	Uruguayan Peso
USSR	Rouble
Venezuela	Bolivar
Vietnam	Dong
Western Samoa	Tala
West Indies Associated States	East Caribbean Dollar (EC$)
Yemen Arab Republic	Yemeni Ryal (also Indian Rupee)
Yemen, People's Democratic Republic of	South Yemen Dinar
Yugoslavia	Yugoslav Dinar
Zaire	Zaire
Zambia	Kwacha (K)

Appendix 16:
Glossary of terms

Actuals: Physical commodities, also commodities readily available. The commodity itself as opposed to a future contract.

Agent: A merchant who acts on behalf of a producer usually on a commission basis.

Anode: The electrode at which negatively charged ions are discharged during electrolysis.

Arbitrage: Operation which consists of selling or buying contracts in one market, simultaneously making the opposite transaction in a different market. A typical *Arbitrage* is a purchase on *COMEX* and a corresponding sale on the LME, or vice-versa.

Backwardation: Market situation in which prices are progressively lower in the future delivery months than in the nearest delivery month. For instance, if the silver quotation for January is 460p per troy oz. and that for March is 457p per troy oz., then the *Backwardation* for two months against January is 3p per troy oz. (*Backwardation* is the opposite of *Contango*.)

Basic price: Agreed price between buyer and seller of an option at which the option may be taken up. Also called the 'striking price'.

Bid: Firm commitment by an interested buyer to pay a stated price (opposite of *Offer*).

Borrowing: Purchase of a nearby delivery date and simultaneous sale of a forward date. Used only on London Metal Exchange.

Broker: Establishes contact between buyer and seller, for a fee. In the US, ring dealing members of futures markets are frequently called brokers.

Bull and Bear: Someone is called a *Bull* when he expects the market to rise and a *Bear* when he expects the market to fall. A *Bull* will usually be *Long*, while a *Bear* will be *Short*.

Bear covering: The act of buying back a speculative *Short* position on a steady or rising market, despite the original intention to await a market drop.

Call: A period for trading. Conducted by a chairman to establish a price for a specific time. During a call, trading is confined to one delivery month.

Call option: The option buyer/taker pays a premium and holds the right to decide at a later stage whether or not to buy at the price agreed at the time the premium was paid. The right may be exercised at any time from the point of purchase to the expiry of the option.

Carrying: General term covering both *Borrowing* and *Lending*.

Carrying Costs: Costs connected with warehouse storage, insurance, etc. On occasion includes interest and estimated changes in weight.

Catalyst: A chemical (metal) which assists a chemical reaction but remains chemically unchanged at the end.

Cathode: The eleetrode at which positively charged (metallic) ions are discharged during electrolysis, hence the slab of metal deposited at the end of the electrolytic process.

C&F: Cost and freight.

CIF: Cost, insurance and freight (included in price).

Clearing house: The organization that provides clearing facilities for some futures markets.

Comex: Usual abbreviation for *Commodity Exchange*, Inc., a New York *Hedge Market* for several commodities, including copper and silver.

Commission house: A company, which trades on behalf of clients for a commission. The *Commission House* only handles clients' business and does not trade on its own account.

Concentrate: The ore of a metal after separation from other unwanted minerals.

Conductivity: A measure of the ability of a metal to conduct an electric current.

Contango: Market situation in which prices are progressively higher in the future delivery months than in the nearest delivery month. For instance, if the *COMEX* silver quotation stands at 457p per troy oz. for January and at 460p per troy oz. for March, then the *Contango* for two months (against January as a basis) is 3p per troy oz. (*Contango* is the opposite of *Backwardation.*)

Contract: An agreement to buy or sell a specified amount of a particular commodity. It details the amount and grade of the product and the date on which the contract will mature and become deliverable, if not previously liquidated.

Contract month: Month in which a given contract becomes deliverable, if not liquidated or traded out before the date specified.

Cover: Purchase of a *Long* contract to offset a previously made sale (see *Liquidation*).

Custom smelter: A smelter which relies on concentrate purchased from independent mines instead of its own captive sources.

Delivery basis: Specified locations to which the commodity in a futures contract may be physically delivered in order to terminate the contract.

Delivery date: Or *Prompt date*, on which the commodity must be delivered to fulfil the terms of the contract.

Delivery month: Calendar month stipulated as month of delivery in a futures contract.

Deposit: Sum of money required by the broker from his client, usually 10 per cent of the value of the contract, to justify opening of a futures position.

Differentials: Premiums paid for grades better than the basic grade, or discounts allowed for grades below the basic grade.

Double option: This is an option which gives the buyer or person taking the option the right either to buy from or sell to the seller of the option or the person who gives it, at the basis price.

Ductility: Quality of a metal by which it may be beaten into sheet or drawn into a wire.

EFP (Exchange For Physical): A trade between two parties wherein one of the parties is the Buyer of the Physicals and the Seller of the Futures Contracts, and the other party is the Seller of the Physicals and a Buyer of the Futures Contracts. Such an *EFP* is made up of four parts: the purchase and sale of Futures contracts coupled with the simultaneous sale and purchase by the same two parties of an equal quantity of the physical commodity. Such transactions may be made at such prices as are mutually agreed upon by the two parties to the transaction.

Electrolysis: A process used for refining metals where the metal is deposited on a cathode from a solution or molten mass.

Element: A substance which cannot be split into anything simpler in a chemical process.

Fabricator: A company which makes semi-fabricated products from refined metal and on occasions from scrap.

Fixation: Fixing price in the future, and used in commodity call purchases and call sale trades.

Flotation: Process by which ore is separated from earth and rubble, during which the ore is introduced to a bath of liquid which is agitated so that the metallic ore either rises to the top or sinks to the bottom.

FOB: Free on Board.

Force Majeure: This is a clause in a supply contract which permits either party not to fulfil the contractual commitments due to events beyond their control. These events may range from strikes to export delays in producing countries.

Forward shipment: Contract covering actual commodity shipments at a specified date in the future.

Futures: Contracts traded for future delivery on a *Hedge* or *Futures Market.*

Futures contract: Contract which requires the delivery of a commodity in a specified future month, if not liquidated before the contract matures.

Futures market: The same as a *Hedge Market*, meaning a market trading in future deliveries, which can also be called a Commodity Exchange or a Terminal Market.

Grades: Standards set for judging the quality of a commodity.

Hall Mark: The official mark or stamp used by gold- and silver-smiths in marking gold and silver articles assayed by them. Also a mark used by government assay offices.

Hedge: A temporary futures market sale made against a physical purchase, or a temporary futures market purchase made against a physical sale, entered into for the purpose of reducing the risk from possible price fluctuations on the physical transaction until the reverse futures market operation cancels the *Hedge* or *Liquidates* the original operation.

Hedge Market: Same as *Futures Market.*

Kerb trading: Unofficial trading when the market has closed. The term 'kerb' dates from the time when dealers continued trading on the kerb outside the exchanges after these had closed.

Last trading day: Final day for trading a particular delivery. Positions which have not been closed by the last trading day must be fulfilled by making, or taking, delivery of the physical commodity or metal.

Lending: Sale of a nearby delivery date coupled with the simultaneous purchase of a more distant date (LME term).

Liquidation: Sale of a *Long* contract to offset a previously made purchase or purchase against a *Short* contract. This term is loosely used for any operation which cancels a previously existing *Position.*

Long: An open purchased futures contract. Buying forward on the market.

Lot: The standard contract unit on a *Hedge* or *Futures Market.* For instance, a silver *Lot* on *COMEX* is 5,000 troy ounces. In practice, the words *Lot, Option,* and *Contract* are interchangeable.

Margin: This is the amount deposited as a guarantee for the fluctuations on a futures purchase or sale. If the contract fluctuates against the holder of the contract, he is required to provide for the difference between his contract price and the current market price by paying 'variation margin' differences. Thus the original margin continues to guarantee fully the performance of the contract at any market price level.

Margin call: A commodity broker's request to a client for additional funds to secure the original deposits.

Nearby delivery: The nearest active month of delivery on a futures market.

Nominal price: An estimated price in the absence of actual transactions. Usually, it is the average between the last *Bid* and the last *Offer.*

Offer: Firm commitment by an interested seller to accept a stated price (opposite of *Bid*).

Open contracts: Contracts bought or sold and not offset by an opposite trade.

Open interest: The total number of contracts, whether purchased or sold, recorded on the books of *COMEX* and which are not offset by the opposite transactions or by physical delivery of the material.

Open outcry: Trading conducted by calling out bids and offers across a ring or pit and having them accepted.

Open position: A forward market position which has not been closed out.

Option: The holder of the option has the right to buy from or sell to the granter of the option a specified quantity of the commodity at an agreed price. The cost of buying the option is known as the premium.

Pegged price: The price at which a commodity has been fixed by agreement.

Plating: The deposition of a layer of a metal on an object forming the cathode during electrolysis.

Position: The *Open Interest* of an individual or firm, as reflected in his books. *Position* also describes the overall status of the purchases and sales of an individual or firm. In this context, one may refer to a Speculative *Position*, a *Hedged Position*, etc.

Position trader: Someone who takes long or short positions in futures markets in consequence of an opinion that prices are about to advance or decline.

Premium: The amount by which a cash commodity price sells over a futures price or another cash commodity price. The excess of one futures contract price over another.

Put option: This option gives the buyer (or 'taker') of the option – in exchange for the premium which he pays – the right to decide at a later date whether or not to sell to the seller (or 'granter') at the price ('basic' or 'striking' price) agreed at the time the premium was paid. The right may be exercised at any point from the purchase of the option up to the declaration date (the date upon which the option expires).

Quotation: Price reported or actually traded on the *LME* or *COMEX*. Also refers to any published or generally known price.

Reduction: A process involving the removal of oxygen or a group which forms negative ions.

Ring: Space on a trading floor where futures are traded. Also known as a pit in the US.

Salt: A compound containing a metal and a non-metal.

Semi-fabrication: The production of metal in the form of wire, sheet, rod etc.

Short: The sale of a commodity not owned by the seller.

Smelt: Extraction of crude metal from the ore by melting, prior to refining.

Sponge: Lumpy form of metal with sponge-like appearance produced by casting molten metal into water.

Spot: Term denoting immediate delivery for cash, as distinct from future delivery.

Spot month: The first month in which delivery can take place and for which a quotation is made on the futures market.

Spot price: The commodity cash sale price, as opposed to a futures price.

Spread: An order to purchase one contract month and sell another month in the same commodity, usually done on the same exchange.

Squeeze: Situation in which those who are *Short* cannot repurchase their contracts, unless at a price substantially higher than the value of these contracts in relation to the rest of the market.

Straddle: The simultaneous buying and selling of the same commodity on the same market. This is designed to take

advantage of differences between two options.
Example – the sale of a September option and the simultaneous purchase of a January option made in the expectation that a later simultaneous purchase of the September and sale of the January options will produce a profit. See *Arbitrage*.

Switch: Change made to an existing *Position* by advancing or postponing the original contract into a different month. This is done by liquidating the original contract and re-establishing the same position by a new purchase or sale, as the case may be.

Switching: Exchanging a commodity in one warehouse for a commodity in another.

Terminal market: Usually synonymous with commodity exchange or futures market, especially in the United Kingdom.

Unwrought: Metal in a cast condition, unworked by mechanical means.

Warrant or Warehouse Receipt: Certificate of physical deposit, which gives title to physical metal in an approved *LME* warehouse and which is recognized good delivery against a *Short Position.* Title to the metal passes when the *Warrant* is endorsed by its current owner to a new owner.

